Street Foods of *Bali*

Street Foods of *Bali*

Heinz von Holzen

Marshall Cavendish
Cuisine

Editor: Sim Ee Waun
Designer: Benson Tan
Photographer: Heinz von Holzen

Published by Marshall Cavendish Cuisine
An imprint of Marshall Cavendish International
1 New Industrial Road, Singapore 536196

Other Marshall Cavendish Offices:

Marshall Cavendish International. PO Box 65829 London EC1P 1NY, UK • Marshall Cavendish Corporation.
99 White Plains Road, Tarrytown NY 10591-9001, USA • Marshall Cavendish International (Thailand)
Co Ltd. 253 Asoke, 12th Flr, Sukhumvit 21 Road, Klongtoey Nua, Wattana, Bangkok 10110, Thailand •
Marshall Cavendish (Malaysia) Sdn Bhd, Times Subang, Lot 46, Subang Hi-Tech Industrial Park, Batu Tiga,
40000 Shah Alam, Selangor Darul Ehsan, Malaysia

Marshall Cavendish is a trademark of Times Publishing Limited

National Library Board, Singapore Cataloguing-in-Publication Data

Holzen, Heinz von.
Street foods of Bali / Heinz von Holzen. – Singapore : Marshall Cavendish Cuisine, c2010.
p. cm.
ISBN-13 : 978-981-261-525-1

1. Cooking, Balinese. 2. Cooking, Indonesian. 3. Snack foods – Indonesia – Bali Island. 4. Cookbooks. I. Title.

TX724.5.I5
641.595986 -- dc22   OCN652345604

Printed in Malaysia by Times Offset (M) Sdn Bhd

Dedication

I'd like to express my deepest respect and gratitude to the countless street vendors, food sellers and proprietors of food outlets in Bali whom I had the pleasure to meet while working on this book. Most of them are never quite certain if they have enough income to cover their daily needs, and yet they have shown me that there is more to life than just the material things. Their natural respect and kindness for one another and the very positive way which they live and embrace life has taught me over and over again that we live on a very beautiful and extremely fragile planet.

Many of the stories in this book were given to me by Mr Fred B. Eisman, also known affectionately to the Balinese as Pak Wayan, a gentleman whom I admire for his decade-long research into the culture of Jimbaran and Bali. His works ensure that the very important cultural elements of this remarkable land is preserved for future generations.

My gratitude also goes to my good friend, Ida Bagus Wisnuwan, our executive chef and one of the first persons I met when I arrived in Bali in 1990. He joined our restaurants a few years ago and is responsible for preparing and testing all the recipes in this book. He was my constant companion in my countless trips all over Bali and other parts of Indonesia in search of street food. His fine personality and in-depth knowledge of Bali's food and culture, together with his terrific skill as a chef contributed much to the colourful and accurate outcome of this book.

I would also like to thank to the ever-growing teams in our various food operations which remain completely dedicated to all the great culinary ventures we are working on. Thank you all for your commitment and support in recording the food culture of Bali.

This book would not be possible without the support of the publishing team at Marshall Cavendish International (Asia), Singapore. Thank you for your expertise, creativity and professionalism in working on this book.

Finally and most importantly, my love, respect and gratitude to my wife Puji and our son Fabian, as well as our family here in Bali, who have steadfastly supported me, stayed on my side and gave me the strength and encouragement to continue my work in various culinary projects. Together, we have learned to respect one another and everything around us. And with this, we cherish the many wonders of Bali and Indonesia.

Heinz von Holzen

Contents

Introduction

About Bali

Bali is a very small island with a land area only slightly over 5,000 square kilometres. Starting at any point in Bali, it is impossible to travel in a constant compass direction for more than about 150 kilometres without reaching the seashore. It is only natural therefore that visitors often make the assumption that the patterns of culture in Bali are uniform from place to place. But nothing can be further from the truth. All the patterns that form the cultural mosaic of Bali vary considerably from one part of the island to the other. These disparate 'micro-cultures' may be at antipodal parts of the island, or they may simply be neighbouring zones in a village and this cookbook reflects that diversity.

Most of Bali's street dishes are simple and utilitarian because food is regarded only as a necessity to the Balinese. While inexpensive and unpretentious, they are at the same time tasty and an absolute joy to eat.

Among the first things visitors to Bali will notice are the countless food stalls along the streets and their patrons having a casual meal standing or squatting alone in a corner. But visitors who hope to find and feast on such local fare in the restaurants and hotels they enter will quickly discover that only very few of such dishes are offered, and it is by far easier to order a pizza or a Caesar salad than the many delicious specialties Indonesia and the island of Bali have to offer. In fact, the average Balinese hardly ever prepares beef or lamb dishes at home on a regular basis, and very seldom, if at all, dines at fine restaurants or hotels frequented by tourists. The foods served in such establishments are specifically prepared with the palate and eating habits of foreign tourists in mind. As we shall see, such tastes and eating habits are quite different than those of the average Balinese.

A Peek Into Warungs

Indeed the short-term visitor to Bali often has very little, if any, contact with everyday Balinese food, for it is unlikely that he would be taken to such *warungs* (casual roadside eateries) by this guide. It can also be tricky for him to find his own way to the *warungs* and navigate the menu enough to know what he is being served. How do you order? What are the foods being served? How is it enjoyed by the locals? What are the little nuances of etiquette among the locals when it comes to food and dining?

This book will provide you not just with the answers to these questions, but also recipes for authentic Balinese cuisine and enticing insights that will give you a deeper understanding of life and the people in Bali through visits to Balinese villages and homes. The dishes featured here are representative of Balinese and Indonesian flavours, and are widely embraced as typical Balinese street food, and are not modified to the palate of Westerners but remain true in taste and presentation.

The book also includes Bali's four renowned dishes: *babi guling* (suckling pig), which requires a proper introduction (page 42) before one truly understands it; *bebek betutu*, widely translated as roast duck in banana leaves, but in truth a steamed dish (page 39); sates, prepared for ceremonies or as a snack, and served with

a dip of chopped chillies and salt (page 46); and lastly, more a genre than a dish, the island's seafood grill—fish, squid and all manner of crustacean cooked over glowing coconut husks and which have given the countless seafood *warungs* along Jimbaran Beach international renown (page 101).

Taste of the Indonesian Archipelago

In exploring the street foods of Bali, you'll also encounter a myriad foods from all over the Indonesian archipelago, now an integral part of Bali's fascinating street food.

With the boom in tourism in the 1990s came the need for more hotels, restaurants and taxis, and with it, the need for more service staff, cooks, travel guides and taxi drivers. This growth brought people from their villages to fast-growing tourist centres like Denpasar, Sanur, Kuta, Jimbaran and Nusa Dua. The influx of workers came not only from Bali but also other parts of Indonesia. They left behind village traditions and practices, and replaced them with six-day work weeks, shift work and the usual pressures of urban life. Far from home and their own hometown flavours, they brought along their beloved foods, resulting in many eateries and fast food outlets sprouting up to cater to the palates of these diverse communities.

These fast food outlets offer a wide selection of dishes, which are prepared and kept warm, then replenished when quantities run low. Such a spread can span various regional cuisines of Indonesia, hence the term *selera nusantara*, loosely translated as "a taste of the Indonesian archipelago". Interestingly, these spreads are often prepared by one chef who may have modified authentic regional flavours to his own native cooking style. As such, dishes from Sumatra, Sulawesi or eastern Indonesia may taste similar to dishes from Java, if the chef hails from Java. Today, these eateries have become popular amongst the local working population, while those with a reputation for good food also attract customers from all levels of society, including the very wealthy.

In featuring these dishes, I have used the original, ethnic names of the various foods and given them English translations. I have also made every effort to use the original plates, dishes, bowls, baskets and other implements that the Balinese use to serve food in. Most dishes pictured in this book were prepared by the actual street vendors and photographed on location. We then took the authentic recipes back to our modern kitchen and with the help of our Balinese and Indonesian chefs, transcribed the recipes—using modern, widely accessible cooking methods and international measurements, so that they can be easily prepared in most homes around the globe.

May you enjoy getting to know Balinese food culture and street food as much as we did working on this book.

Dining Etiquette

Selamat makan means "enjoy your meal". It is a greeting used before a meal throughout Indonesia.

In Bali, meals almost always revolve around rice. In fact, rice accounts for 75 per cent of any one meal by weight alone. A typical meal will consist of a mound of freshly cooked rice and small amounts of two or three other dishes as an accompaniment to the rice. In fact, in the Indonesian language, the name for any side dish is made up of the name of the food and the term "*daaran nasi*", which means "food eaten with rice". Such accompanying dishes may be fish or meat, vegetables, or a soy bean dish such as fermented soy bean cakes (*tempe*) or tofu.

Traditionally, the Balinese and most Indonesians eat without cutlery, using only the right hand. The left hand is considered unclean because it is used for ablutions.

The technique to manoeuvre the food depends on whether the main ingredient, the rice, is steamed (*nasi kuskus*) or boiled (*nasi jakan*). Steamed rice can be easily moulded into a convenient shape while boiled rice is less sticky and cannot be moulded.

In general, the average Balinese family, for reasons of economy, consumes very little meat or fish for their daily meals. Meat may account for about 15 per cent of a family's daily expenses, fish may be a little less and rice may be about 30 per cent.

Vegetables are cultivated and animals are reared in the home compound as additional sources of income. Almost every household in the villages has its clutter of chickens underfoot and pigs sleeping in the shade. You'll also find fishermen on every sandy beach and banana and coconut trees on every square metre of arable land. The produce is brought to the market and sold to purchase household necessities.

Invitation to Dinner

While many other cultures view meals as a social event, it is not a commonly held custom among the Balinese to invite guests for a meal at home as a pre-planned social gathering. Visitors may drop in to discuss important matters or just to chat. They may then be offered coffee or tea and a snack, but business is never transacted over meals. It is not a habit to have working breakfasts or lunches.

If guests are present when the host would like to eat, they are always asked to join him, but this offer is routinely declined. Eating out with friends as a social event is also traditionally uncommon among the Balinese. They, themselves may eat a meal away from home, but usually only when necessary, such as when they are away from home for work. The preference is always to eat at home.

Basic Recipes & Condiments

Shallot & Lemongrass Dressing *Sambel Matah*

Ingredients

Shallots 40 g (1⅓ oz), peeled and finely sliced

Lemongrass 75 g (2⅔ oz), ends trimmed, bruised and finely sliced

Garlic 20 g (⅔ oz), peeled and finely chopped

Bird's eye chillies 30 g (1 oz), finely sliced

Kaffir lime leaves 2, finely chopped

Dried prawn (shrimp) paste (*terasi*) ½ tsp, toasted and finely crumbled

Lime juice 2 Tbsp, freshly squeezed

Coconut oil 4 Tbsp

Salt a pinch

Ground black pepper a pinch

Preparation

1. Combine all ingredients in a deep bowl and mix thoroughly for 5 minutes.

2. Adjust seasoning with more salt and pepper if necessary.

NOTE

Another way of preparing this dressing is to cook it. To cook this dressing, heat oil in a heavy saucepan and add all the ingredients. Sauté for about 5 minutes over medium heat or until sauce is fragrant. Cool to room temperature before serving.

Fried Chilli Dressing

Sambel Sere Tabia

Ingredients

Vegetable oil 4 Tbsp

Shallots 100 g (3⅓ oz), peeled and finely sliced

Garlic 75 g (2⅔ oz), peeled and finely chopped

Bird's eye chillies 30 g (1 oz), finely sliced

Dried prawn (shrimp) paste (*terasi*) ½ tsp, roasted and finely crumbled

Salt a pinch

Preparation

1. Heat oil in a frying pan. Add shallots and garlic and sauté for 2 minutes.

2. Add chillies and prawn paste and continue to sauté until golden.

3. Season with salt.

Dried Fish & Cucumbers in Lime Dressing *Sambal Teri*

Indonesians like their dishes spicy and would add substantial amounts of chilli to this dressing. Vary the amount of chilli added according to your personal taste. Bird's eye chillies, while small, can be very potent!

Ingredients

Vegetable oil 2 Tbsp

Garlic 5 cloves, peeled and sliced

Dried anchovies 100 g (3^1/$_3$ oz), rinsed and drained

Cucumber 1, medium, peeled, seeded and sliced

Salt 1 Tbsp

Coconut ^{1}/$_4$, grated and toasted

Bird's eye chillies 2–5, finely sliced

Crushed black pepper a pinch

Coriander seeds 1 tsp, roasted and finely crushed

Lime juice 3 Tbsp

Preparation

1. Heat oil in a saucepan. Add garlic and dried anchovies and sauté until very fragrant. Cool to room temperature.

2. Combine sliced cucumbers and 1 Tbsp salt and mix well. Leave to marinate in a cool place for 20 minutes. (This process breaks down the fibres causing the cucumber to release a lot of water.)

3. Wash cucumbers thoroughly under running water. Drain well and pat dry.

4. Mix all ingredients in a bowl, season to taste with salt, pepper and lime juice.

Green Chilli Sambal *Sambal Lado Hijau*

Ingredients

Vegetable oil 3 Tbsp

Shallots 50 g (1^2/$_3$ oz), peeled and sliced

Large green (or red) chillies 100 g (3^1/$_3$ oz), halved, seeded and sliced

Bird's eye chillies 3–6

Plum tomatoes 100 g (3^1/$_3$ oz), skinned, halved, seeded and sliced

Kaffir lime leaves 3

Lime juice 1 Tbsp

Salt to taste

Preparation

1. Combine shallots and chillies in a stone mortar or food processor, and grind into a fine paste.

2. Heat oil in heavy saucepan. Add ground shallots, chillies and kaffir lime leaves and sauté over medium heat for five minutes.

3. Add tomatoes and continue to sauté for 2–3 more minutes over low heat.

4. Season to taste with lime juice and salt.

Spicy Crisp-fried Anchovies *Sambal Teri*

Ingredients

Vegetable oil for frying

Dried anchovies 300 g (10 oz), heads removed and cleaned

Large red chillies 50 g (1²/₃ oz), halved lengthwise, seeded and sliced

Plum tomatoes 100 g (3¹/₃ oz), skinned, seeded and diced

Lime juice 2 Tbsp

Lemon basil a few sprigs

Spice Paste

Vegetable oil 2 Tbsp

Shallots 30 g (1 oz), peeled and sliced

Garlic 20 g (²/₃ oz), peeled and sliced

Ginger 30 g (1 oz), peeled and sliced

Bird's eye chillies 4–8, according to taste

Large red chillies 40 g (1¹/₃ oz), halved lengthwise, seeded and sliced

Crushed white pepper a pinch

Palm sugar 3 Tbsp

Preparation

1. Heat oil in pan and fry anchovies until golden and crispy. Drain and set aside.

2. Prepare spice paste. Combine all ingredients in stone mortar or food processor and grind into a fine paste.

3. Heat oil in heavy saucepan. Add ground spice paste and sliced chillies and sauté until fragrant.

4. Increase heat, add anchovies and stir fry until anchovies are evenly coated with the spices.

5. Add diced tomatoes, mix well.

6. Season with lime juice and garnish with lemon basil. Serve as a topping on fried rice and noodle dishes or as a side dish with other dishes and rice.

Fried Garlic
Kesuna Goreng

Ingredients

Garlic 100 g (3¹/₃ oz), peeled and thinly sliced
Vegetable oil 4 Tbsp

Preparation

1. Dry garlic on paper towels.
2. Heat oil until moderately hot, then add garlic and fry until lightly golden.
3. Remove and drain well on paper towels before using or storing in an airtight container.

Fried Shallots
Bawang Goreng

Ingredients

Shallots 100 g (3¹/₃ oz), peeled and thinly sliced
Vegetable oil 4 Tbsp

Preparation

1. Dry shallots on paper towels.
2. Heat oil until moderately hot, then add shallots and fry until lightly golden.
3. Remove and drain well on paper towels before using or storing in an airtight container.

Spice Pastes

Almost every cooking process in Indonesia starts with the grinding of spices into spice pastes, which forms the basis of many dishes. Travelling from region to region in Indonesia, you will notice great differences in flavours and composition of these aromatic spice mixes, ranging from a handful of spices to a complex blend as prepared on the island of Bali. These marinades can be prepared in advance in larger quantities, and then cooled overnight in the refrigerator, packed into smaller portions and frozen for later use. If properly stored, these spice pastes will last for months.

The local markets are where you will find a great many varieties of spices used in everyday cooking. One important point to keep in mind when shopping for spices is the fact that the appearance, aroma, flavour, texture and effectiveness of a given spice can vary greatly depending on factors such as when the spice was harvested, the weather and season, and soil conditions. Select spices that are unblemished and smell fresh, and do not store them for too long.

Spiced Tomato Sauce I
Sambal Tomat

Ingredients

Vegetable oil 90 ml (3 fl oz / $^3/_8$ cup)

Shallots 90 g (3¼ oz), peeled and sliced

Garlic 50 g (1$^2/_3$ oz), peeled and sliced

Large red chillies 180 g (6$^1/_2$ oz), seeded and sliced

Bird's eye chillies 180 g (6$^1/_2$ oz)

Dried prawn (shrimp) paste (*terasi*) 1 Tbsp, roasted

Palm sugar 20 g ($^2/_3$ oz), chopped

Tomatoes 350 g (12 oz), very ripe, peeled and seeded

Lime juice 1 Tbsp

Salt to taste

Preparation

1. Heat oil in heavy saucepan. Add shallots and garlic and sauté until golden.

2. Add chillies and continue to sauté until chillies are soft.

3. Add palm sugar and prawn paste and continue to sauté until sugar caramelises.

4. Add tomatoes and continue to sauté until tomatoes are soft. Set aside to cool.

5. When cool enough to handle, place it in a stone mortar or food processor and grind coarsely.

6. Season to taste with salt and lemon juice.

Spiced Tomato Sauce II
Sambal Tomat Padas

Ingredients

Vegetable oil 3 Tbsp

Bird's eye chillies 50 g (1$^2/_3$ oz)

Dried prawn (shrimp) paste (*terasi*) 1 tsp, roasted and finely crumbled

Palm sugar 1 tsp

Tomatoes 200 g (7 oz), skinned and seeded

Lime juice 2 Tbsp

Salt to taste

Crushed black pepper to taste

Preparation

1. Heat oil in heavy saucepan. Add bird's eye chillies and sauté over medium heat until just soft.

2. Add prawn paste and palm sugar and continue to sauté until chillies are soft.

3. Add tomatoes and continue to sauté for 2 minutes. Set aside and cool.

4. Place cooked ingredients into a stone mortar and grind into a coarse paste.

5. Season to taste with lime juice, salt and pepper.

Spice Paste for Seafood
Base Be Pasih

Ingredients

Large red chillies 450 g (1 lb), halved, seeded and sliced

Garlic 50 g (1²/₃ oz), peeled and sliced

Shallots 225 g (7¹/₂ oz), peeled and sliced

Turmeric 175 g (6 oz), peeled and sliced

Ginger 100 g (3¹/₃ oz), peeled and sliced

Candlenuts 125 g (4¹/₂ oz)

Tomato 1, about 200 g (6¹/₂ oz), halved and seeded

Coriander seeds 2 Tbsp, crushed

Dried prawn (shrimp) paste (*terasi*) 2 Tbsp, roasted

Coconut oil 125 ml (4 fl oz / ¹/₂ cup)

Salt ³/₄ Tbsp

Tamarind pulp 2¹/₂ Tbsp, seeds and fibre removed

Water 250 ml (8 fl oz / 1 cup)

***Salam* leaves** 3

Lemongrass 2 stalks, ends trimmed, bruised

Preparation

1. Combine all ingredients except salt, tamarind pulp, water, salam leaves and lemongrass in a mortar or food processor and grind coarsely.

2. Place ground ingredients in a heavy saucepan, add remaining ingredients and simmer over medium heat for about 1 hour or until water has evaporated and marinade changes to a golden colour.

3. Set aside to cool before using.

NOTE

Make up a large batch of stock, then freeze in small containers and thaw the required amount when needed.

Spice Paste for Chicken
Base be Siap

Ingredients

Bird's eye chillies 50 g (1²/₃ oz), finely sliced

Garlic 125 g (4¹/₂ oz), peeled and sliced

Shallots 225 g (7¹/₂ oz), peeled and sliced

Lesser galangal (*kencur*) 50 g (1²/₃ oz), peeled and finely sliced

Galangal 60 g (2 oz), peeled and sliced

Turmeric 125 g (4¹/₂ oz), peeled and sliced

Candlenuts 100 g (3¹/₃ oz)

Palm sugar 50 g (1²/₃ oz), chopped

Coconut oil 150 ml (5 fl oz / ²/₃ cup)

Lemongrass 2 stalks, ends trimmed, bruised

***Salam* leaves** 3

Water 250 ml (8 fl oz / 1 cup)

Salt ³/₄ Tbsp

Preparation

1. Combine all ingredients except lemongrass, *salam* leaves, water and salt in a stone mortar or food processor and grind coarsely.

2. Place ground ingredients in a heavy saucepan, add remaining ingredients and simmer over medium heat for about 1 hour or until water has evaporated and marinade changes to a golden colour.

3. Set aside to cool before using.

Spice Paste for Beef
Base be Sampi

Ingredients

Large red chillies 250 g (9 oz), halved, seeded and sliced

Bird's eye chillies 40 g (1¹⁄₃ oz), finely sliced

Garlic 50 g (1²⁄₃ oz), peeled and sliced

Shallots 200 g (7 oz), peeled and sliced

Ginger 50 g (1²⁄₃ oz), peeled and sliced

Galangal 150 g (5¹⁄₃ oz), peeled and chopped

Candlenuts 100 g (3¹⁄₃ oz)

Crushed black pepper 2 Tbsp

Coriander seeds 2 Tbsp, crushed

Palm sugar 40 g (1¹⁄₃ oz), chopped

Coconut oil 150 ml (5 fl oz / ²⁄₃ cup)

Salam **leaves** 3

Water 250 ml (8 fl oz / 1 cup)

Salt ³⁄₄ Tbsp

Preparation

1. Combine all ingredients except *salam* leaves, water and salt in a stone mortar or food processor and grind coarsely.

2. Place ground ingredients in a heavy saucepan, add remaining ingredients and simmer over medium heat for about 1 hour or until water has evaporated and marinade changes to a golden colour.

3. Set aside to cool before using.

Stock
Kuah

Ingredients

Chicken or duck carcass, beef or pork bones 5 kg (11 lb 2 oz), chopped into small pieces

Spice paste (use according to type of stock, pages 26–27) 1¹⁄₂ cups

Lemongrass 1 stalk, ends trimmed and bruised

Kaffir lime leaves 3, torn

Large red chillies 2, bruised

Bird's eye chillies 3

Salam **leaves** 2

Crushed white pepper 1 Tbsp

Coriander seeds 1 Tbsp, crushed

Preparation

1. Rinse bones until water runs clear, then place in a stockpot and cover with cold water. Bring to boil over high heat. Drain and discard water. Wash bones again under running water.

2. Place bones into a larger stockpot, add three times as much water as bones and return to a boil. Reduce heat and add all other ingredients and simmer stock over very low heat for 5–6 hours. Remove scum as it accumulates.

3. It is important not to cover the stockpot during cooking as it will make the stock cloudy. Strain stock before using.

Balinese Peanut Sauce

Ingredients

Bird's eye chillies 6, sliced

Garlic 5 cloves, peeled and sliced

Lesser galangal (*kencur*) 50 g (1²/₃ oz), peeled and sliced

Raw peanuts with skin 500 g (1 lb 1¹/₂ oz), deep-fried or roasted

Palm sugar 50 g (1²/₃ oz), chopped

Sweet soy sauce (*kicap manis*) 4 Tbsp

Water 300 ml (10 fl oz / 1¹/₄ cups), or as needed

Lime juice 1 Tbsp

Salt a pinch

Preparation

1. Using a mortar, pound chillies into a very fine paste.

2. Add garlic, lesser galangal and peanuts and continue to pound into a very fine paste. Add palm sugar and sweet soy sauce.

3. Gradually add water and slowly work paste into a creamy dressing, adding water as required.

4. Season to taste with lime juice and salt. Serve warm.

NOTE

As a result of grinding the small chillies to a fine paste, you get a very spicy sauce. If it is too spicy for your taste, simply reduce the number of chillies or replace with a large red chilli. This sauce can also be made in a food processor, although the real flavour will only be achieved by working a little harder with a stone mortar.

Javanese Peanut Sauce

Ingredients

Raw peanuts with skin 500 g (1 lb 1¹/₂ oz), toasted

Garlic 5 cloves, peeled and sliced

Bird's eye chillies 6–10, according to taste, sliced

Lesser galangal (*kencur*) 50 g (1²/₃ oz), peeled and sliced

Dried prawn (shrimp) paste (*terasi*) ¹/₂ tsp

Coconut milk 1 litre (32 fl oz / 4 cups)

Sweet soy sauce (*kicap manis*) 4 Tbsp

Palm sugar 50 g (1²/₃ oz), chopped

Tamarind pulp 1 Tbsp, seeds and fibre removed

Kaffir lime leaves 2, torn

Lime juice 1 Tbsp

Salt a pinch

Fried shallots (page 23) 1 Tbsp

Preparation

1. Combine peanuts, garlic, chillies and lesser galangal in a food processor or stone mortar and grind to a fine paste.

2. Place paste into a heavy saucepan with coconut milk, sweet soy sauce, palm sugar, tamarind pulp and lime leaves. Bring to boil, then reduce heat and simmer uncovered, stirring frequently for 10 minutes to prevent sauce from sticking to the bottom of the pot.

3. Season to taste with lime juice and salt. Garnish with fried shallots just before serving. Serve warm.

NOTE

For storing or freezing: If you wish to make a larger quantity of this sauce for freezing, follow steps 1 and 2 above, but omit the coconut milk. Mix this thick paste well, then press it into ice cube trays and freeze. Once the paste is frozen, remove from tray, pack into airtight containers or a freezer bag. When required, simply take the cubes from the freezer, thaw for 20 minutes, add coconut milk and bring to the boil, then simmer for 10 minutes. Do not freeze sauce once coconut milk is added as coconut milk will curdle easily or turn sour very quickly when reheated.

Rice Cakes

For certain purposes, rice is prepared in the form of cakes known as *ketipat* or *lontong*. These rice cakes comprise a woven wrapper called *urung*, made from pale green palm leaves or banana leaves in the case of *lontong*, into which uncooked rice is packed and then boiled.

There are many different shapes of rice cakes, the more exotic of which are used for religious ceremonies. The most common type, called by various names such as *ketipat nasi*, *ketipat biasa* or *ketipat bekel*, is simply a flattened square pocket with convex sides.

Why rice cakes? Firstly, rice cooked in leaves is always softer than steamed or boiled rice. Secondly, rice prepared as a parcel is easy to carry. This is the standard means by which cooked rice is carried by a farmer to the fields for a snack or hauled around by the many push cart hawkers in Bali. Thirdly, cooked in leaves, the rice can be prepared a little overcooked so that it is softer, easier to chew and digest by the elderly. In this case, it is called *ketipat nyaling*, meaning "slippery". Interestingly, prolonged cooking of rice produces porridge, but when wrapped in leaves, it merely becomes soft cooked rice.

To cook rice cakes, wash the rice just as you are going to cook it in the usual manner. Fill the leaf parcel half-full with rice and boil for a few hours. The rice cake is ready when no water runs out when you lift the parcels out of the boiling water.

Lontong

Ingredients

Glutinous rice 300 g (10 oz), soaked for 10 minutes

Vegetable oil 3 Tbsp

Shallots 50 g (1²/₃ oz), peeled and sliced

Garlic 20 g (²/₃ oz)

Ginger 20 g (²/₃ oz)

Lesser galangal (*kencur*) 20 g (²/₃ oz), peeled and sliced

Lemongrass 1 stalk, ends trimmed and bruised

Kaffir lime leaves 2

Coconut milk 600 ml (20 fl oz / 2¹/₂ cups)

Salt a pinch

Banana leaves as needed, cut into sheets about 25 x 15-cm (10 x 6-in)

NOTE

If banana leaves are not available, replace with plastic wrap or even aluminum foil. For a lighter version, replace coconut milk with chicken or vegetable stock.

Preparation

1. Wash rice thoroughly under running water. Drain.

2. Combine shallots, garlic, galangal and ginger in a stone mortar and grind to a fine paste.

3. Heat oil in heavy saucepan, add the ground paste, lemongrass and kaffir lime leaves. Sauté over medium heat for 2 minutes or until fragrant.

4. Add rice and continue to sauté until rice is evenly coated with the paste.

5. Top up with coconut milk, add salt, mix well, and bring to boil. Reduce heat and simmer while continuously stirring until most of the liquid is absorbed and rice starts to dry up. Set aside and cool to room temperature.

6. Place 3 heaped tablespoonfuls of rice in the centre of each banana leaf and roll up tightly. Fasten with bamboo skewers or toothpicks and secure with butcher string. Repeat until rice is used up.

7. Steam parcels for 30 minutes. Allow to cool before serving.

Local Markets

There is no other place that captures the local colour, buzz and atmosphere of Bali as well as the markets scattered throughout the island. Balinese markets are colourful, vivid, buzzing centres of social life. It has been said that the roadside *warung* is the domain of Balinese men and the village market is the realm of the women.

At the markets, you will find everything that the island has to offer, from fresh produce such as meat, poultry, seafood, eggs, vegetables and spices, to essential utensils for the Balinese kitchen, a great variety of snacks and cakes ever so loved by the locals, and even ready-prepared meals consisting of rice and accompaniments. (The long, sausage-shaped banana leaf parcels are typically filled with fish, while bag-shaped packages contain meat and the oversized ones both fish and meat.)

Most markets on the island are in full swing from the very early morning hours. During this time, the markets exude a sense of vibrance and freshness which tapers off as the morning progresses.

As many villagers have no refrigeration at home, it is impossible to keep food fresh for a long time. As such, food is purchased fresh, ready to use only for that day. This also means that almost all products at the market are incredibly fresh. Vegetables are normally harvested the day before and then distributed by small trucks overnight to the countless markets around the island where they will be sold in the early morning hours. While vegetables make it from the farm to the table within 24 hours, most meat is freshly butchered on the same morning it is sold at the market. Ice, to this day, is still a rare sight in most markets.

Basic clothing is also available from the markets, ranging from children's clothes to a great range of *sarongs*, shorts and T-shirts. Even medication for headaches and sores are sold, together with many herbs used in traditional herbal medicine. In some markets, there are even shops selling gold jewellery.

Lining the main roads next to the markets are usually countless food carts that offer the busy and hungry early morning shoppers a range of popular breakfast foods, ranging from black rice pudding (*bubuh injin*), to one of Indonesia's most popular snacks, mung bean porridge (*bubuh kacang ijo*). In the same parking area, one will also find the strange looking bicycles completely laden with toys and candies.

Bearing in mind the relatively small daily budgets that the locals come shopping with—about US$3 to US$4 —you'll be fascinated by the incredible range of goods available here. But where items sold at supermarkets tend to be packaged in larger portions, the opposite takes place in the market. Everything from shampoos to instant noodles can be found in small quantities, enough for just the day's consumption.

It is a communal effort that keeps these markets going. Every stall holder is required to pay a small tax that goes partly to the government and partly to the village community fund which, in turn, pays for the upkeep of these remarkable marketplaces.

Iconic Bali

Ducks

The scene of a duck herd guiding his flock to the fields, or *sawah* in the early morning, then back home in the late afternoon is a Balinese classic. A common sight, ducks are often raised in areas where there are irrigated rice fields. But in the drier parts of Bali where there are no irrigated fields, one almost never sees ducks either in the fields or the markets.

There is a feeling among the Balinese that the duck is inherently a more intelligent animal than the chicken. While chickens run around helter-skelter eating whatever they find, ducks stick together, are rather particular about what they eat, and thrive happily in water and on land. It is this long-held view that leads the Balinese to prefer duck meat to chicken meat. Indeed, Balinese people who will not eat beef or pork for various personal or religious reasons generally prefer duck to chicken. Having said that, duck is not a common meat at the table for the average Balinese family. When it is cooked at home, it is likely to be cooked the same way as chicken is. Interestingly though, farmers here generally raise ducks for their eggs rather than for meat.

The one classic Balinese dish that tourists will invariably encounter is *bebek betutu*. The mix of fiery spices and strong flavours are rubbed all over the bird which is then wrapped in betel nut leaves which completely seal in the flavours and slow cooked for 8 to 10 hours. The result is simply incredible. Juicy meat falls off the bone, and when dipped into the duck's juices and mixed with a little spice marinade and rice, makes a perfect meal fit for a king!

Roast Duck in Banana Leaf
Bebek Betutu

Ingredients

Duck 1 whole, about 2 kg (4 lb 6 oz)

Salt to taste

Crushed black pepper to taste

Tapioca, cassava or spinach leaves 200 g (7 oz), cleaned, blanched for 5 minutes and roughly chopped

Salam **leaves** 4

Bamboo skewers as needed

Vegetable oil 3 Tbsp + more for brushing duck

Banana leaves for wrapping

Stuffing

Shallots 70 g (2$^1/_3$ oz), peeled and sliced

Garlic 30 g (1 oz), peeled and sliced

Ginger 40 g (1$^1/_3$ oz), peeled and sliced

Turmeric 40 g (1$^1/_3$ oz), peeled and sliced

Lesser galangal (*kencur*) 30 g (1 oz), washed and sliced

Galangal 30 g (1 oz), peeled and sliced

Candlenuts 30 g (1 oz), crushed

Bird's eye chillies 4–7, according to taste, sliced

Crushed black pepper 1 tsp

Coriander seeds 1 tsp, crushed

Dried prawn (shrimp) paste (*terasi*) 2 tsp, roasted and coarsely crushed

Lemongrass 3 stalks, ends trimmed, finely sliced

Kaffir lime leaves 5, finely chopped

Salt a pinch

NOTE

You can also cook the duck in your crockpot, slow cooker, or oven at a cool temperature.

Preparation

1. Place all stuffing ingredients in stone mortar or food processor and grind into a coarse paste.

2. Place one-third of the paste in a bowl, add 3 Tbsp vegetable oil and mix well. Set aside the remaining two-thirds of the paste.

3. Wash duck and pat dry. Season inside and out with salt and pepper.

4. Combine tapioca and *salam* leaves with two-thirds of the paste. Stuff into cavity of duck.

5. Work remaining stuffing under the skin of duck breast which prevents the breast from drying out during cooking. Close cavity with skewers.

6. Brush the outside of the duck with some oil.

7. Wrap duck in several layers of banana leaves and fasten ends with bamboo skewers. Steam for 1$^1/_2$ hours.

8. Open the top layer of the banana leaves to expose the top. Bake the duck in a preheated oven at 160°C (325°F) for 30–40 minutes, or until duck is cooked and golden brown.

9. Unwrap, cut meat into small pieces and serve with stuffing on the side.

Crispy Fried Duck
Calokok Bebek

Ingredients

Duck 1, about 2 kg (4¹/₂ lb), cut into 8 pieces

Vegetable oil 2 Tbsp + more for deep-frying

Lemongrass 2 stalks, ends trimmed and bruised

Cinnamon stick 5 cm (2 in) length

Salam **leaf** 1

Chicken or duck stock (page 23) 2 litres (64 fl oz / 8 cups)

Salt a pinch

Crushed black pepper a pinch

Rice flour 1 cup

Marinade

Large red chilies 85 g (3 oz), halved, seeded and sliced

Shallots 150 g (5 oz), peeled and sliced

Garlic 40 g (1¹/₃ oz), peeled and sliced

Ginger 30 g (1 oz), peeled and sliced

Lesser galangal (*kencur*) 30 g (1 oz), sliced

Turmeric 60 g (2 oz), peeled and sliced

Candlenuts 30 g (1 oz), crushed

Dried prawn (shrimp) paste (*terasi*) 1 tsp, roasted

Coriander seeds 1 tsp, crushed

Crushed black pepper ¹/₄ tsp

Grated nutmeg ¹/₂ tsp

Cloves 5, crushed

Vegetable oil 4 Tbsp

Lemongrass 1 stalk, ends trimmed and bruised

Salam **leaf** 1

Salt ¹/₄ tsp

Water 4 Tbsp

Preparation

1. Prepare marinade. Combine all ingredients except oil, lemongrass, *salam* leaf and water in a mortar or food processor and grind into a fine paste.

2. Place paste in a heavy saucepan, add remaining marinade ingredients and simmer over medium heat until all the liquid has evaporated and sauce is fragrant and golden shiny. Set aside to cool before using.

3. Marinate duck with 125 g (4¹/₂ oz / ¹/₂ cup) marinade for 1 hour in a cool place.

4. Heat oil in heavy saucepan. Add another 125 g (4¹/₂ oz / ¹/₂ cup) marinade, lemongrass, cinnamon and *salam* leaf and sauté for about 2 minutes.

5. Add stock and bring to the boil, then lower heat and simmer for 1 minute.

6. Add marinated duck pieces and return to a boil. Lower heat and simmer for 30–40 minutes until duck is almost cooked. Remove saucepan from heat and leave duck to cool in pan.

7. When cooled to room temperature, remove duck from stock and pat dry.

8. Heat oil in a wok for deep-frying.

9. Season duck pieces with another 125 g (4¹/₂ oz / ¹/₂ cup) marinade, salt and pepper. Dust evenly with rice flour, then deep-fry in medium hot oil until duck is crispy and golden brown.

10. Drain well and serve.

42

Babi Guling

Babi guling is perhaps one of the most well known Balinese dishes, and which travel guides almost always translate as "roast suckling pig". A typical serving comprises a few slices of *babi guling* served on top of a generous serving of rice and garnished with crispy pork skin. Together with it are traditional accompaniments including a banana stem soup (*jukut ares*), braised pork ribs (*balung nangka*), green bean pork salad (*lawar kacang*), slices of fried pork sausage (*urutan*), a couple of pork sates (*sate celeng*) and most importantly, a dip or two of fiery chilli sauce.

As synonymous as it is with Bali, the average Balinese very seldom cooks or eats pork at home, except on ceremonial occasions. Pigs are large animals, and to slaughter an entire pig just for home consumption is expensive. So most Balinese head to the *warungs* to buy a plate of *babi guling*, or with an advance order, the entire pig. Here, a plate of *babi guling* is about Rp10,000 to Rp20,000 (US$1.20 to US$2.50), far beyond the budget of the average Balinese.

Most *warungs* sell freshly roasted pigs that weigh between 25 kg and 35 kg. These young animals are freshly slaughtered, cleaned, filled with spices and stuffing and slowly roasted. This results in a very tasty and rather spicy dish. However, the meat can be somewhat tough—something the foreign visitor will have to get used to when partaking of it.

Roast Pig
Babi Guling

Ingredients

Suckling pig 1, 6–8 kg

Salt 1¹/₂ Tbsp

Shallots 200 g (7 oz), peeled and sliced

Garlic 100 g (3¹/₃ oz), peeled and sliced

Ginger 100 g (3¹/₃ oz), peeled and chopped

Turmeric 350 g (12 oz), peeled and chopped

Candlenuts 250 g (9 oz), chopped

Galangal 100 g (3¹/₃ oz), peeled and finely chopped

Bird's eye chillies 120 g (4 oz), sliced

Lemongrass 10 stalks, ends trimmed and finely sliced

Coriander seeds 3 Tbsp, crushed

Crushed black pepper 1 Tbsp

Dried prawn (shrimp) paste *(terasi)* 1 Tbsp, roasted and crumbed

Kaffir lime leaves 5, finely chopped

Salam **leaves** 2

Cassava leaves 800 g (1³/₄ lb), rinsed, then blanched for 5 minutes and roughly sliced

Vegetable oil for basting

Turmeric Water

Turmeric 125 g (4¹/₂ oz), peeled and finely chopped

Water 250 ml (8 fl oz / 1 cup)

NOTE

If you have a large barbecue with rotisserie or constantly turning spit, you can cook the pig over charcoal for an authentic Balinese flavour.

Preparation

1. Clean suckling pig thoroughly inside and out. Season well with salt, including cavity.

2. Combine all other ingredients, except cassava leaves, oil and turmeric water, in a food processor or stone mortar and grind coarsely into a paste.

3. Combine paste with cassava leaves. Mix well.

4. Fill cavity of pig with cassava mixture and close belly with kitchen string or bamboo skewers.

5. Prepare turmeric water. Blend turmeric with water and use this to brush pig skin until it is shiny and yellow.

6. Place pig on a roasting rack and roast in a preheated oven at 160°C (325°F) for 3–4 hours. Baste frequently with oil.

7. When pig is done, let it rest in a warm place for 20 minutes before serving.

8. When serving, first remove the crisp skin with a strong carving knife, then loosen meat from the bones and cut into slices. Place a heaped tablespoon of stuffing on each serving plate and top with meat and skin.

Braised Oxtail Stew with Leeks *Rawon Buntut*

Getting hold of the Indonesian black nuts can be a challenge outside of Southeast Asia. When you have found them, crack open the nut—just as you would open a walnut—then remove and grind up the meat.

Ingredients

Oxtail 1.2 kg (2 lb 10 oz), cut in 2.5-cm (1-in) slices

Beef stock (page 23) 1.5 litres (48 fl oz / 6 cups)

Vegetable oil 3 Tbsp

Indonesian black nut meat 80 g (2^1/$_2$ oz), finely ground

Tamarind pulp 1 Tbsp, mixed with 3 Tbsp warm water and strained

Lemongrass 3 stalks, ends trimmed and bruised

Kaffir lime leaves 6, bruised

Leek or spring onions (scallions) 200 g (7 oz), white part only, sliced

Salt and pepper to taste

Bean sprouts 100 g (3^1/$_3$ oz)

Chinese celery leaves 30 g (1 oz), sliced

Fried shallots (page 23) 2 Tbsp

Spice Paste

Shallots 60 g (2 oz), peeled and sliced

Garlic 40 g (1^1/$_3$ oz), peeled and sliced

Turmeric 30 g (1 oz), peeled and sliced

Ginger 10 g (^{1}/$_2$ oz), peeled and sliced

Galangal 10 g (^{1}/$_2$ oz), peeled and sliced

Candlenuts 40 g (1^1/$_3$ oz)

Lemongrass 1 stalk, ends trimmed, bruised and finely sliced

Coriander seeds 1 tsp, roasted and finely crushed

Cumin 1 tsp

Sweet soy sauce (*kecap manis*) 1 Tbsp

Palm sugar 1 tsp, chopped

Salt 1 tsp

Vegetable oil 1 Tbsp

Beef stock (page 23) 125 ml (4 fl oz / ^{1}/$_2$ cup)

Garnish

Fermented soy bean cake (*tempe*) 200 g (7 oz), sliced and deep-fried

Prawn crackers (page 56) a handful, fried

Spiced tomato sauce I (page 25) 4 Tbsp

Duck eggs 4, hardboiled

Preparation

1. Rinse oxtail well. Place in a pot and cover with water. Bring to boil over high heat. Drain and rinse oxtail until water runs clear. Drain again and allow oxtail to drip dry.

2. Bring beef stock to boil in a saucepan and keep it simmering until ready to use.

3. Prepare spice paste. Place all spice paste ingredients in a mortar or a food processor and grind to a fine paste. Set aside.

4. Heat vegetable oil in a heavy saucepan. Add spice paste, black nut meat, tamarind juice, lemongrass and kaffir lime leaves and sauté over medium heat until fragrant. Add oxtail and sauté until evenly coated with paste.

5. Add half the simmering beef stock, reduce heat and slowly braise oxtail until meat is very tender and almost falls off the bone. Takes 2–3 hours. Add more beef stock in small quantities during braising as the liquid evaporates.

6. When done, remove oxtail and strain sauce back into a pot. Return oxtail to pot and add leek or spring onions. Simmer for another 5 minutes. Season to taste with salt and pepper.

7. Arrange oxtail in a deep soup bowl, pour over the sauce and sprinkle with bean sprouts, celery leaves and fried shallots.

8. Serve hot with garnish on a separate plate and steamed rice or *lontong* (page 31).

Sate

For most visitors to Bali, these richly flavoured meat skewers taste best served with a creamy peanut sauce similar to that served in certain parts of Indonesia. The locals however prefer sate served dipped in a mixture of salt and chopped chillies.

Made mostly made from pork or chicken, sates are normally marinated with a complex spice paste, *base gede*, for about 15 minutes to an hour before being skewered on sticks and grilled over coconut husk charcoal. As this charcoal does not burn well unless fanned vigorously, grilling is a two-fisted job—sate sticks in the left hand and fan in the right.

Unlike the sate served in hotels and restaurants, the traditional sate found in markets and *warungs* all over Bali are likely to have sinew, gristle, fat and skin, which is what the locals are used to eating when it comes to sate. Whenever sate is prepared, the *tukan sate* (sate seller) will first thread a chunk of pork belly or fat on the wooden sate skewer before adding the marinated meat.

As street stalls do not have the luxury of refrigeration, the various meats for sate are always made from fresh marinated meat. The marinade not only acts as a flavouring for the meat, but also as an agent to preserve the meat.

There are two main types of sate in Bali—sate *asam*, sate *lilit* or *lembat*. Sate *asam* is either made from pork or chicken, and is likely to be full of fat, skin and gristle. Sate *lilit* or *lembat* is perhaps Bali's most original sate. It is made from a mixture of very finely chopped pork, chicken or duck meat, grated coconut, spices and sometimes coconut milk, wrapped around a flattened bamboo stick. It is typically grilled over a coconut shell charcoal fire by inserting the ends of the sticks into a piece of banana that serves as a holder for the sate while they are being cooked. One can find many food stalls along the road from Sanur towards Klungkung which specialise in selling this type of this very tasty sate but mostly made from various fish such as tuna, marlin or mackerel.

One reason why sate is always freshly prepared and served directly from the grill is because they will be dry and tough if served cold. Sate is also always grilled over very hot charcoal so the palm sugar in the marinade will caramelise and give the sate a lovely flavour and aroma.

Balinese Seafood Sate
Sate Ikan Laut

Pak Nyoman, the sate seller, together with his wife Ketut, usually start preparing their tasty sates around noon. On a typical day, they can sell up to 20 kg (44 lb) of sate. Seven sticks per serving together with rice cakes, a dip of salt mixed with chopped chillies, and a very spicy tomato chilli sauce, make this a perfect mid day snack!

Ingredients

Skinned boneless fish fillet 800 g (1³/₄ lb), cut into 2.5-cm (1-in) cubes

Bird's eye chillies 3–5, according to taste finely chopped

Palm sugar 2 Tbsp

Salt to taste

Bamboo skewers as needed

Marinade

Large red chillies 150 g (5¹/₃ oz), halved, seeded and sliced

Garlic 30 g (1 oz), peeled and sliced

Shallots 80 g (2⁴/₅ oz), peeled and sliced

Turmeric 60 g (2 oz), peeled and sliced

Ginger 30 g (1 oz), peeled and sliced

Candlenuts 40 g (1¹/₃ oz)

Tomatoes 70 g (2¹/₃ oz), halved and seeded

Coriander seeds 1 tsp

Dried prawn (shrimp) paste (*terasi*) 1 tsp, roasted

Salt 1 tsp

Vegetable oil 2 Tbsp

Tamarind pulp 1 Tbsp, seeds and fibre removed

***Salam* leaf** 1

Lemongrass 1 stalk, ends trimmed, bruised

Water 4 Tbsp

Preparation

1. Prepare marinade. Combine all ingredients except vegetable oil, tamarind pulp, *salam* leaf, lemongrass and water in a stone mortar or food processor and grind into a fine paste.

2. Place ground ingredients in a heavy saucepan, and add remaining marinade ingredients. Simmer over medium heat until all the liquid has evaporated and sauce is fragrant, shiny and golden. Set aside to cool.

3. Reserve a quarter of ground paste for basting mix.

4. Combine fish cubes with 125 g (4¹/₂ oz) of marinade, bird's eye chillies, palm sugar and salt. Mix well.

5. Skewer 4–5 cubes of fish tightly onto each skewer until all have been used up.

6. Combine another 100 g (3¹/₃ oz) of ground paste with 100 ml (3¹/₃ fl oz / 6 Tbsp) vegetable oil and mix well. Use as a basting mix.

7. Grill sates over very hot charcoal until golden brown, basting often. Serve hot.

NOTE

You can also use beef or lamb to make the sate. Follow the same directions as above.

Minced Fish Sate
Sate Languan

Ingredients

Skinned boneless fish fillet 800 g (1³/₄ lb),
finely minced or chopped

Coconut milk 125 ml (4 fl oz / ¹/₂ cup)

Kaffir lime leaves 5, finely chopped

Palm sugar 1 Tbsp

Crushed black pepper a pinch

Salt a pinch

Large bamboo skewers or lemongrass stalks
as needed

Marinade

Large red chillies 100 g (3¹/₃ oz), halved,
seeded and sliced

Bird's eye chillies 3–5, according to taste, sliced

Garlic 30 g (1 oz), peeled and sliced

Shallots 80 g (2⁴/₅ oz), peeled and sliced

Turmeric 60 g (2 oz), peeled and sliced

Ginger 30 g (1 oz), peeled and sliced

Candlenuts 40 g (1¹/₃ oz)

Tomatoes 70 g (2¹/₃ oz), halved and seeded

Coriander seeds 1 tsp

Dried prawn (shrimp) paste (*terasi*) 1 tsp, roasted

Coconut oil 2 Tbsp

Tamarind pulp 1 Tbsp, seeds and fibre removed

***Salam* leaf** 1

Lemongrass 1 stalk, ends trimmed, bruised

Water 100 ml (3¹/₂ fl oz / 6 Tbsp)

Preparation

1. Prepare marinade. Combine all ingredients
   except coconut oil, tamarind pulp, *salam* leaf,
   lemongrass and water in a stone mortar or food
   processor and grind into a fine paste.

2. Transfer paste to a heavy saucepan, add
   remaining marinade ingredients and simmer
   over medium heat until all the liquid has
   evaporated and sauce is fragrant, shiny and
   golden. Set aside to cool.

3. Combine minced fish, coconut milk, kaffir lime
   leaves, palm sugar, pepper and salt and 125 ml
   (4 fl oz / ¹/₂ cup) cooked marinade in a mixing
   bowl. Mix into a homogenous sticky paste.

4. Mould a heaped tablespoonful of minced
   fish mixture around a wooden skewer or over
   trimmed stalks of lemongrass.

5. Combine remaining paste with an equal amount
   of vegetable oil. Mix well and use as a baste
   when grilling sates.

6. Grill fish sate over very hot charcoal until golden
   brown, basting frequently to prevent them from
   burning and drying out. Basting will also give
   the sate a beautiful golden colour. Serve hot.

Chicken Sate
Sate Madura

This popular street snack is found all over the island whenever there is a gathering of people. You find them outside most markets, near bus stops and schools, food courts and wherever there is a ceremony or cock-fighting competition. These flavoursome sates are always prepared to order and eaten on the spot, which make them a safe street snack for the visitor. A delicate sweet sate, it is mostly served with *ketipat* (rice cakes), slices of shallots and lime wedges. Accompanying them is a peanut dipping sauce which is sweetened with a generous amount of sweet soy sauce.

Ingredients

Chicken breast 800 g (1³/₄ lb), cut into small cubes

Sweet soy sauce (*kicap manis*) 200 ml (6¹/₂ fl oz / ⁴/₅ cup)

Coriander seeds 1 tsp, roasted and crushed

Crushed black pepper ¹/₂ tsp

Lime juice 2 Tbsp

Shallots 100 g (3¹/₃ oz), peeled and quartered

Limes 2, cut into wedges

Bamboo skewers as needed

Lontong **(page 31)** 1 quantity

Javanese or Balinese Peanut sauce (page 28) 1 quantity

NOTE

This sate is often served with slices of shallots, lime wedges and rice cakes and with a peanut dipping sauce that is sweetened with a generous amount of sweet soy sauce. You can also use beef or lamb to make the sate. Follow the same directions as above.

Preparation

1. Combine sweet soy sauce, coriander, black pepper and lime juice in a bowl and mix well.
2. Add chicken cubes and leave to marinate for about 30 minutes.
3. Thread chicken cubes through bamboo skewers.
4. Grill sate over very hot charcoal and baste.
5. When done, serve hot with rice cakes and peanut sauce.

Pork Sate
Sate Asam Celeng

Ingredients

Pork neck 600 g (1 lb 5^1/$_3$ oz), cut into small cubes
Bird's eye chillies 3–5, chopped
Palm sugar 1 Tbsp
Salt a pinch

Marinade

Large red chillies 75 g (2^2/$_3$ oz), halved, seeded and sliced
Shallots 125 g (4^1/$_2$ oz), peeled and sliced
Garlic 30 g (1 oz), peeled and sliced
Ginger 20 g (^{2}/$_3$ oz), peeled and sliced
Lesser galangal (*kencur*) 30 g (1 oz), sliced
Turmeric 50 g (1^2/$_3$ oz), peeled and sliced
Candlenuts 20 g (^{2}/$_3$ oz), crushed
Dried prawn (shrimp) paste (*terasi*) 1 tsp, roasted
Coriander seeds 1 tsp, crushed
Crushed black pepper ^{1}/$_4$ tsp
Grated nutmeg ^{1}/$_4$ tsp
Cloves 4, crushed
Vegetable oil 4 Tbsp
Lemongrass 1 stalk, ends trimmed, bruised
***Salam* leaf** 1
Salt ^{1}/$_4$ tsp
Water 4 Tbsp

NOTE

Always serve sates directly from the grill. Never cook them in advance as they will turn dry and tough and lose its flavour. Whenever possible, grill over very hot charcoal. The charcoal should be so hot that it almost burns the meat skewers. This way, the palm sugar in the marinade will caramelise, lightly burn and add the desired flavour.

Preparation

1. Prepare marinade. Combine all ingredients, except vegetable oil, lemongrass, *salam* leaf and water, in a stone mortar or food processor and grind into a fine paste.

2. Heat oil in a heavy saucepan. Add paste and remaining marinade ingredients and simmer over medium heat until all the liquid has evaporated and sauce is fragrant. Set aside to cool.

3. Combine meat, chillies, palm sugar and salt with 125 g (4^1/$_2$ oz) marinade and mix well.

4. Skewer 4–6 cubes of meat securely on a bamboo skewer until ingredients are used up. Set aside.

5. Meanwhile, combine remaining marinade with an equal amount of vegetable oil. Set aside as basting mix.

6. Grill sates over very hot charcoals, basting them frequently. This will prevent the spices from burning and help the flavour penetrate the meat.

7. Serve hot.

Lamb Sate
Sate Kambing

Ingredients

Boneless lamb 800 g (1³/₄ lb), cut into small cubes

Salt 1 tsp

Bamboo skewers as needed

Vegetable oil 2 Tbsp

Shallots 70 g (2¹/₂ oz)

Garlic 50 g (1²/₃ oz), peeled and sliced

Coriander seeds 1 Tbsp, roasted

Crushed black pepper ¹/₂ tsp

Sweet soy sauce (*kicap manis*) 125 ml (4 fl oz / ¹/₂ cup)

Preparation

1. Season lamb cubes with salt, then thread onto bamboo skewers.

2. Heat oil in a heavy saucepan. Add shallots and sauté until soft.

3. Combine softened shallots, garlic, coriander seeds and pepper in a stone mortar and grind into a fine paste. Add sweet soy sauce and mix until smooth.

4. Dip sate into soy sauce mixture and let excess sauce drip off.

5. Grill over hot charcoal, frequently basting with remaining sauce.

6. Serve sate hot with remaining sauce as a dip.

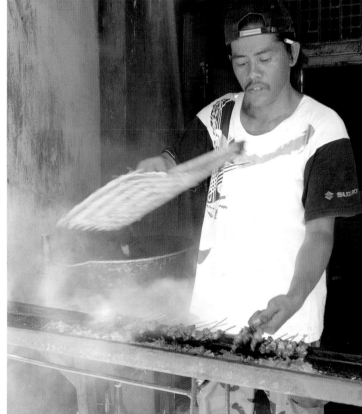

Juket Pecel

Many mixed vegetable dishes in Bali are prepared in more or less standard combinations. They are commonly sold in *warungs* either to be eaten on the spot or taken home to be shared with the family. Sellers of such mixed vegetable dishes are also a common sight outside the larger markets in Denpasar. They often set up temporary stalls in the parking lots next to markets or spread their wares out on the pavement.

The vegetable mixture that is most familiar outside of Bali is similar to the popular Indonesian dish known as *gado-gado,* which is a standard on most Indonesian hotel menus in some form or another. The Balinese version is called *jukut plecing* or *jukut pecel.* There is no one standard recipe for *pecel,* just as there is no one for *gado-gado.* Basically *jukut plecing* consists of a mixture of spices and boiled vegetables. The list of vegetables almost always includes water spinach and cabbage. Together with it may be long beans, spinach, and bean sprouts.

The spice mixture is prepared separately in a large stone mortar and poured over the vegetables when it is served.

Vegetable Salad with Spicy Peanut Sauce
Pecel

Ingredients

Water spinach 150 g (5$^1/_3$ oz), washed and cut into 2-cm ($^3/_4$-in) lengths

Bean sprouts 150 g (5$^1/_3$ oz), picked and washed

Long beans or string beans 200 g (7 oz), cut into 2.5-cm (1-in) lengths

Sauce

Garlic 4, peeled and sliced

Shallots 5, peeled and sliced

Large red chillies 2 halved, seeded and sliced

Bird's eye chillies 3–6, according to taste

Lesser galangal (*kencur*) 20 g ($^2/_3$ oz), peeled and sliced

Turmeric 20 g ($^2/_3$ oz), cleaned and sliced

Dried prawn (shrimp) paste (*terasi*) 1 tsp, roasted

Tamarind pulp 4 Tbsp, seeds and fibre removed

Kaffir lime leaves 3, finely chopped

Peanuts with skin 250 g (9 oz), deep-fried or roasted

Warm water as needed

Salt to taste

Topping

Fried shallots (page 23) 3 Tbsp

Raw peanuts with skin 50 g (1$^2/_3$ oz), roasted and crushed

Fermented soy bean cake (*tempe*) 200 g (7 oz), sliced and deep-fried

Hard-boiled eggs 2, peeled and sliced

Lemon basil 20 g ($^2/_3$ oz)

Vegetable crackers as desired

Preparation

1. Blanch or steam each vegetable separately, taking care not to overcook them. Drain well and dry on a paper towel.

2. To make the sauce, heat a little oil in a saucepan and stir-fry garlic, shallots, chillies, lesser galangal and turmeric until golden and fragrant.

3. Transfer to a stone mortar or food processor. Add prawn paste, kaffir lime leaves and peanuts, and pound coarsely, gradually adding tamarind pulp and enough water to make a smooth sauce.

4. Place cooked vegetables in a deep bowl; then add enough sauce to coat. Mix well.

5. Arrange salad in a deep serving dish and top with fried shallots, crushed peanuts, fermented soy bean cake, hard-boiled eggs and lemon basil. Serve.

Kripik & Krupuk

Crackers or chips are immensely popular snacks in Bali and there are two main types: *kripik* and *krupuk*.

Kripik is almost always made from slicing ingredients thinly and deep-frying them. And the ingredients can range from fruit or tubers, chicken, pork skin, internal organs or snails imported from Java. As *kripik* is made from fresh, untreated produce, these chips cannot be stored for long.

Krupuk is made from processing fruit, roots or tubers and kneading it into dough. The dough is then rolled into cylinders, steamed, sliced very thin, then thoroughly dried, usually in the sun. These *krupuk* slices can be kept for a long time, and are fried in very hot oil only before serving. One of the most common varieties of *krupuk* is *krupuk udang,* made from cassava starch and a finely ground powder of dried prawns (shrimps). Alternatively, the additive can be powdered dried fish of various kinds, which is known as *krupuk ikan. Krupuk* can also be made with garlic, shallots, vegetables or even from the seeds of fruit.

Besides making a tasty snack, *kripik* and *krupuk* offer a good solution to prolong the shelf life of food that may otherwise quickly deteriorate. Cassava is a good example. Once harvested, cassava root lasts only about a week before it starts to spoil. Chopped into small pieces and dried, cassava chips can be stored for a long time.

Peanut Crackers
Rempeyek Kacang

Ingredients

Raw peanuts with skin 200 g (7 oz), toasted
Rice flour 50 g (1²/₃ oz)
Cake flour 100 g (3¹/₃ oz)
Coconut milk 375 ml (12 fl oz / 1¹/₂ cups)
Vegetable oil for deep-frying

Spice Paste

Peanut oil 1 Tbsp
Garlic 20 g (²/₃ oz), peeled and chopped
Turmeric 30 g (1 oz), peeled and chopped
Kaffir lime leaves 5, finely chopped
Candlenuts 10 g (¹/₃ oz), crushed
Coriander seeds 1 tsp, roasted
Salt to taste

Preparation

1. Wrap peanuts in a paper towel and rub gently to remove skins.
2. Place ingredients for spice paste in a stone mortar or food processor and grind into a fine paste.
3. Place spice paste and rice and cake flours in a deep bowl and mix well.
4. Gradually stir in coconut milk and mix into a runny batter.
5. Stir in peanuts.
6. Heat oil in a wok. Drop in 1 Tbsp batter at a time and fry until golden brown. Drain well on paper towels. Store in an airtight container.

Green Bean Crackers
Krupuk Ijo

Ingredients

Coriander seeds 1 tsp, roasted

Cashew nuts 5, roasted

Garlic cloves 2

Salt a pinch

Egg 1

Coconut milk 250 ml (8 fl oz / 1 cup)

Rice flour 80 g (2²/₃ oz)

Tapioca flour 60 g (2 oz)

Mung beans 250 g (9 oz), soaked in water for
   at least 8 hours and drained

Vegetable oil for frying

Preparation

1. Combine coriander seeds, cashew nuts, garlic
   and salt in stone mortar and grind into a fine
   paste. Transfer to a mixing bowl.

2. Mix in egg and coconut milk.

3. Add rice and tapioca flours and mix into a
   smooth batter.

4. Stir in mung beans. Mix thoroughly.

5. Heat oil in a shallow pan until moderately hot.
   Drop spoonfuls of batter into the oil and fry
   until crackers are golden and crisp. Drain on
   paper towels and store in an airtight container.

Prawn Crackers
Krupuk Udang

Ingredients

Prawns (shrimps) 300 g (10 oz), peeled and minced

Garlic 30 g (1 oz), peeled and finely chopped

Plain (all-purpose) flour 250 g (9 oz)

Cassava flour 1 kg (2 lb 3 oz)

Hot water 1.5 litres (32 fl oz / 4 cups)

Salt to taste

Baking soda 1 tsp

Preparation

1. Combine all ingredients to form a dough.
   Knead thoroughly, then roll dough into
   70 x 5-cm (30 x 2-in) cylinders.

2. Place dough on wooden racks and into a
   steamer. Steam for 30–60 minutes.

3. Set aside steamed rolls to cool for 1–2 days.

4. Slice thinly and dry in the sun. Store in an
   airtight container.

5. Deep-fry slices in very hot oil when required.

Padang Food

Padang food in Indonesia can be likened to what Italian food is on the global food scene. It is the richly spiced food from West Sumatra, and you'll find at least one Padang restaurant in every town in Indonesia. Some are decent, others are very good and some are outstandingly delicious.

So what is this cuisine like? Some dishes are fiery hot and others can be on the heavy side, as most dishes are smothered in coconut milk. If there is an imperial cuisine in Indonesia, then Padang cuisine will most likely be it. The popularity of Padang cuisine spread over the centuries as West Sumatrans travelled across the Indonesian archipelago and settled in every corner of the land, even in the most remote and isolated places. In many of the Padang restaurants here in Bali, one might still encounter some Padang cooks that recently settled in Bali, though most of the Padang cooks are second or third generation residents of Bali.

Another reason for the popularity of Padang food is the belief that Padang dishes are not only delicious, but they can also be reheated several times. Because of this belief, however, the quality and standard of Padang food varies widely from restaurant to restaurant: freshly cooked Padang dishes can be fantastically tasty, but sometimes the dishes can be several days old, having been re-heated many times over!

A Padang restaurant hardly offers guests a menu. Once guests are seated, a waiter will place countless dishes of food on the table, followed by a plate of steaming rice for each customer. It is up to you what you want to eat and they will only be charged for the dishes consumed. Whatever is left on the plates are returned to the pot where it will be served again. None of the dishes are served hot, and many are dark-coloured and look unappetising. But what they lack in looks, they make up for in taste and flavour!

If you are tempted to try a Padang restaurant, head to busy roadside *warungs* with a high turnover. Try to be there just after the breakfast crowd at around 10 o'clock, when you can be almost certain that most dishes are freshly cooked and have not sat behind a glass window for hours waiting for a hungry customer.

Warung Cuisine

Hot & Sour Seafood Soup
Ikan Asam Padas

Ingredients

Whole firm fish (red mullet, snapper, mackerel)
1, about 800 g (1³/₄ lb), cleaned and sliced evenly

Salt and pepper to taste

Lime juice 2 Tbsp

Chicken stock (page 23) 1 litre (32 fl oz / 4 cups)

Tomatoes 4, medium, peeled, seeded and
sliced in wedges

Spice Paste

Vegetable oil 3 Tbsp

Large red chillies 60 g (2 oz) halved, seeded and
sliced

Bird's eye chillies 5–7, according to taste, sliced

Shallots 80 g (2⁴/₅ oz), peeled and sliced

Garlic 40 g (1¹/₃ oz), peeled and sliced

Galangal 30 g (1 oz), peeled and sliced in fine stripes

Turmeric 30 g (1 oz), peeled and sliced

Ginger 30 g (1 oz), peeled and sliced

Sour starfruit 5, sliced

Kaffir lime leaves 3

***Salam* leaves** 2

Lemongrass 2 stalks, ends trimmed, bruised and
finely sliced

Garnish

Lemon basil 12 sprigs, roughly sliced

Sour starfruit 5, halved and sliced

NOTE

As a variation to this recipe, use 800 g (1³/₄ lb) mixed seafood such as prawns, squid and clams.

Preparation

1. Season fish with salt, pepper and lime juice. Leave to marinate.

2. Prepare spice paste. Combine all spice paste ingredients except kaffir lime leaves, *salam* leaves and lemongrass in a stone mortar or food processor and grind into a fine paste.

3. Heat some oil in a heavy saucepan. Add spice paste, kaffir lime leaves, *salam* leaves and lemongrass, and sauté until fragrant.

4. Add stock and bring to a boil, then turn down heat and let it simmer for 1 minute.

5. Add fish and leave to simmer until fish is tender.

6. Carefully remove fish from stock and arrange in a serving bowl.

7. Add tomatoes to stock. Return to a simmer, then season with salt and pepper.

8. To serve, scatter garnish over fish, then pour over soup.

Beef Soup with Black Nuts *Rawon Surabaya*

Ingredients

Vegetable oil 2 Tbsp

Lemongrass 2 stalks, ends trimmed, bruised

Kaffir lime leaves 3, torn

Beef brisket or shoulder 800 g (1³/₄ lb), cut into small cubes

Beef stock (page 23) 1.5 litres (48 fl oz / 6 cups)

Salt to taste

Ground black pepper to taste

Spring onions (scallions) 3 Tbsp, sliced

Fried shallots (page 23) 3 Tbsp

Spice Paste

Shallots 50 g (1²/₃ oz), peeled and sliced

Garlic 40 g (1¹/₃ oz), peeled and sliced

Turmeric 30 g (1 oz), peeled and sliced

Galangal 20 g (²/₃ oz), peeled and sliced

Dried prawn (shrimp) paste (*terasi*) 1 tsp, roasted

Coriander seeds 1 Tbsp, roasted and crushed

Palm sugar 1 Tbsp

Sweet soy sauce (*kicap manis*) 1 Tbsp

Indonesian black nuts 3–4, shelled and blanched until tender

Tamarind pulp 2 Tbsp, seeds and fibre removed

Preparation

1. Prepare spice paste. Place shallots, garlic, turmeric, galangal, prawn paste and coriander seeds in a stone mortar or food processor and grind into a fine paste.

2. Add palm sugar, soy sauce, black nuts and tamarind pulp and continue to grind until smooth.

3. Heat oil in a heavy saucepan. Add spice paste, lemongrass and kaffir lime leaves and sauté over medium heat until fragrant.

4. Add beef cubes and continue to sauté until meat changes colour.

5. Add beef stock and bring to a boil. Reduce heat and simmer until meat is tender. This can take several hours. Ensure that there is always plenty of stock or water in the saucepan in which the meat can simmer.

6. Season with salt and black pepper. Dish out and garnish with spring onions and fried shallots. Serve hot.

Nasi Campur

Nasi campur refers to a meal of rice with a variety of side dishes often sold at a *warung*. In such *warung*s, there is usually a glass display case neatly piled with plates of pre-cooked dishes. When a *nasi campur* meal is ordered at the *warung*, the proprietor, usually a woman, would scoop a large mound of cooked rice onto a serving plate, then add small amounts of each of the pre-cooked dishes onto the plate, finally topping it off with a spoonful of *sambal* (spicy chilli sauce).

Such *warung*s also do a thriving business selling *nasi bungkus,* which is simply *nasi campur* sold in a packet for takeaway. The typical packaging is conical and almost invariably made out of a banana leaf or two. The rice and accompanying dishes are placed in the cone, which is then folded over to cover the contents, and the package secured with a sliver of bamboo. People going on picnics or to a distant temple for worship often bring along huge baskets of *nasi bungkus* for lunch after their prayers.

Grilled Chicken Lombok
Ayam Panggang

Ingredients

Spring chickens 4, each about 800 g (1³/₄ lb)
Vegetable oil 2 Tbsp

Marinade

Bird's eye chillies 7
Shallots 70 g (2¹/₃ oz) , peeled and sliced
Garlic 50 g (1²/₃ oz), peeled and sliced
Lesser galangal (*kencur*) 40 g (1¹/₃ oz)
Galangal 50 g (1²/₃ oz)
Turmeric 60 g (2 oz)
Candlenuts 45 g (1¹/₂ oz)
Palm sugar 30 g (1 oz)
Dried prawn (shrimp) paste (*terasi*) 1 tsp
Lemongrass 1 stalk, ends trimmed
***Salam* leaf** 1
Kaffir lime leaf 1
Chicken stock (page 23) 500 ml (16 fl oz / 2 cups)
Coconut milk 500 ml (16 fl oz / 2 cups)

NOTE

As a variation to this recipe, try deep-frying the marinated chickens instead of grilling them.

Preparation

1. Split chickens in half along the back bone. Cut them open butterfly-style and flatten out.
2. Prepare marinade. Combine chillies, shallots, garlic, both types of galangal, turmeric, candlenuts, palm sugar and prawn paste in a stone mortar or food processor and grind to a fine paste.
3. Heat oil in saucepan. Add ground spices, lemongrass, *salam* and kaffir lime leaves and sauté over low heat until fragrant.
4. Prepare a basting mix. Transfer a quarter of the marinade into a bowl and combine with an equal amount of vegetable oil.
5. Place chicken stock, coconut milk and remaining marinade in a saucepan and bring to a boil. Reduce heat and simmer for 2 minutes.
6. Add chickens and simmer until almost cooked. Remove saucepan from the heat and leave chickens to cool to room temperature in sauce.
7. Remove chickens from sauce and leave them to dry. Reserve the sauce.
8. Season dried chickens with salt and pepper and grill over very hot charcoal until golden brown. Baste with basting mix frequently on both sides.
9. Return reserved sauce to a simmer and reduce until all the liquid has evaporated for a dipping sauce to go with chicken.
10. Serve hot with rice and a condiment of choice (pages 20–21).

Padang Chicken Curry
Gulai Padah Ajam

Ingredients

Chicken 1, about 1.2 kg (2^1/$_2$ lb), cut into 8 pieces

Tamarind pulp 2 Tbsp, soaked for 10 minutes in 100 ml (3^1/$_3$ fl oz / 6 Tbsp) warm water, then strained; reserve tamarind liquid

Vegetable oil 3 Tbsp

Lemongrass 2 stalks, ends trimmed, bruised

Kaffir lime leaves 3

Turmeric leaf 1, sliced

Coconut milk 1 litre (32 fl oz / 4 cups)

Salt and pepper to taste

Spice Paste

Shallots 50 g (1^2/$_3$ oz), peeled and sliced

Garlic 30 g (1 oz), peeled and sliced

Large red chillies 70 g (2^1/$_3$ oz), halved, seeded and sliced

Candlenuts 20 g (^{2}/$_3$ oz), crushed

Turmeric 30 g (1 oz), peeled and sliced

Ginger 30 g (1 oz), peeled and sliced

Preparation

1. Combine chicken pieces with tamarind water. Mix well and leave to marinate for 30 minutes.

2. Make spice paste. Combine all ingredients and grind in a stone mortar or food processor into a fine paste.

3. Heat oil in a heavy saucepan. Add spice paste, lemongrass, kaffir lime leaves and turmeric leaf and sauté over medium heat until fragrant.

4. Add coconut milk and bring to a boil.

5. Add chicken pieces and return to a boil. Reduce heat and simmer over very low heat until chicken is tender.

6. Season with salt and pepper to taste. Serve hot with rice and a condiment of choice (pages 20–21).

Fried Chicken in Sweet Onion Sauce
Ayam Goreng Kecap Manis

Ingredients

Whole chicken 1, about 1.2 kg (2¹/₂ lb) cut into 8 pieces

Salt ¹/₂ tsp

Ground black pepper ¹/₂ tsp

Plain (all-purpose) flour 50 g (1²/₃ oz)

Vegetable oil for deep-frying

Sauce

Vegetable oil 2 Tbsp

Shallots 60 g (2 oz), peeled and sliced

Garlic 60 g (2 oz), peeled and sliced

Onion 100 g (3¹/₃ oz), peeled and sliced

Spring onions (scallions) or leeks 50 g (1²/₃ oz), cut into short lengths

Large red chillies 60 g (2 oz), halved, seeded and sliced

Tomato 1, medium, peeled and cut into wedges

Sweet soy sauce (*kicap manis*) 3 Tbsp

Salty soy sauce (*kicap asin*) 1¹/₂ Tbsp

Salt and pepper to taste

Preparation

1. Season chicken with salt and pepper, then dust evenly with flour.

2. Heat oil in a wok. When oil is hot and smoking, lower heat and leave oil to cool until about 140°C (275°F).

3. Lower in chicken. Cook in batches if wok is small. Deep-fry chicken slowly until golden and crispy. Remove and drain well.

4. Prepare sauce. Heat oil in a saucepan, then add shallots, garlic, onion, spring onions or leeks and chillies. Sauté over medium heat until soft. Add tomato and continue to sauté for another minute.

5. Mix in the soy sauces and sauté for another minute. Season to taste with salt and pepper.

6. Pour sauce over chicken. Serve hot with rice and a condiment of choice (pages 20–21).

Prawns Braised in Spicy Chilli Sauce
Sambal Udang

Ingredients

Large prawns (shrimps) 800 g (1³/₄ lb), peeled and deveined, leaving tails intact

Lime juice 2 Tbsp

Salt and pepper to taste

Vegetable oil 2 Tbsp

Petai 100 g (3¹/₃ oz), halved

Coconut milk 200 ml (6¹/₂ fl oz / ⁴/₅ cup)

Tamarind pulp 2 Tbsp, soaked for 10 minutes in 100 ml (3¹/₃ fl oz / 6 Tbsp) warm water, then strained; reserve tamarind liquid

Large plum tomato 1, peeled, seeded and sliced into small wedges

Spice Paste

Shallots 30 g (1 oz), peeled and sliced

Garlic 20 g (²/₃ oz), peeled and sliced

Turmeric 20 g (²/₃ oz), peeled and sliced

Ginger 20 g (²/₃ oz), peeled and sliced

Large red chillies 100 g (3¹/₃ oz), halved, seeded and sliced

Bird's eye chillies 2–4, according to taste, sliced

Dried prawn (shrimp) paste (*terasi*) ¹/₂ tsp, roasted

Sugar 1 tsp

Large plum tomato 1, peeled, seeded and coarsely chopped

NOTE

If *petai* is not available, substitute with any other fresh beans such as red beans, black beans or borlotti beans.

Preparation

1. Season prawns with lime juice, salt and pepper and marinate for 10 minutes.

2. Prepare spice paste. Combine all ingredients except tomato in a mortar or food processor and grind into a fine paste. Stir in chopped tomato.

3. Heat oil in a heavy saucepan and sauté spice paste until fragrant.

4. Add prawns and *petai* and sauté until evenly coated with spice paste.

5. Add coconut milk and bring to a boil, then simmer until sauce thickens.

6. Add tamarind liquid and mix well. Add tomato wedges and heat through.

7. Dish out and serve hot with rice and a condiment of choice (pages 20–21).

Corn and Fern Tips in Coconut Sauce
Gulai Jagung-Pakis

Ingredients

Prawns (shrimps) 200 g (7 oz), peeled and cleaned

Vegetable stock or water 250 ml (8 fl oz / 1 cup)

Coconut cream 125 ml (4 fl oz / ¹⁄₂ cup)

Corn kernels 300 g (10 oz), blanched

Fern tips 300 g (10 oz), washed, cut into short lengths and blanched

Salt and pepper to taste

Limes 2–3, halved

Spice Paste

Bird's eye chillies 6–10, according to taste, sliced

Shallots 50 g (1²⁄₃ oz), peeled and sliced

Garlic 30 g (1 oz), peeled and sliced

Turmeric 30 g (1 oz), peeled and sliced

Ginger 30 g (1 oz), peeled and sliced

Galangal 20 g (²⁄₃ oz), peeled and sliced

Cardamom pods ¹⁄₂ tsp, peeled and crushed

Cumin ¹⁄₂ tsp

Cloves 4, crushed

Crushed white pepper ¹⁄₂ tsp

Vegetable oil 2 Tbsp

Cinnamon stick 1, about 10-cm (4-in) long

NOTE

Fern tips can be substituted with asparagus or spinach.

Preparation

1. Prepare spice paste. Combine all ingredients except the oil and cinnamon in a stone mortar or food processor and grind into a fine paste.

2. Heat oil in heavy saucepan. Add paste and cinnamon and sauté over medium heat until fragrant.

3. Add prawns and mix well. Sauté for 1 minute.

4. Add stock or water and coconut cream and bring slowly to boil.

5. Add corn kernels and fern tips and return to the boil. Lower heat and simmer for 2 minutes.

6. Season to taste with salt and pepper and a generous squeeze of lime juice.

7. Dish out and serve hot with rice and a condiment of choice (pages 20–21).

Potato & Meat Patties
Perkedel Kentang

Ingredients

Vegetable oil 4 Tbsp

Potatoes 300 g (10 oz), peeled and cut in 3-cm (1¼-in) cubes

Chicken leg 300 g (10 oz), minced

Eggs 3, beaten

Chinese celery 30 g (1 oz), roughly chopped

Spring onions (scallions) 30 g (1 oz), sliced

Salt and pepper to taste

Rice flour for dusting

Spice Paste

Shallots 40 g (1⅓ oz), peeled and sliced

Bird's eye chillies 2, sliced

Ground nutmeg ½ tsp

Egg Wash

Eggs 2, beaten

Preparation

1. Prepare spice paste. Combine all spice paste ingredients in a mortar or food processor and grind into a fine paste.

2. Heat 2 Tbsp oil in a heavy saucepan. Add spice paste and sauté over medium heat until fragrant. Set aside to cool.

3. Place potatoes in a steamer and steam until soft. Remove and set aside on a tray to let the excess moisture escape.

4. Push potatoes through a fine sieve to mash.

5. Combine minced chicken, spice paste, potatoes, eggs, Chinese celery and spring onions in a bowl and mix into a paste. Season with salt and pepper.

6. Form mixture into individual patties 3 cm (1¼ in) in diameter and 1.5-cm (¾-in) thick.

7. Dust each pattie with a little rice flour, then dip in egg wash.

8. Heat remaining 2 Tbsp oil in a frying pan and pan-fry patties until golden.

9. Serve hot with rice and a condiment of choice (pages 20–21).

Eggs Braised in Spiced Coconut Milk
Gulai Telur

Ingredients

Vegetable oil 2 Tbsp

Turmeric or pandan leaf 1

Coconut milk 500 ml (16 fl oz / 2 cups)

Eggs 8, hard-boiled and peeled

Salt and pepper to taste

Spice Paste

Shallots 50 g (1²/₃ oz), peeled and sliced

Garlic 30 g (1 oz), peeled and sliced

Large red chillies 70 g (2¹/₃ oz), halved seeded and sliced

Ginger 30 g (1 oz), peeled and sliced

Turmeric 30 g (1 oz), peeled and sliced

Galangal 30 g (1 oz), peeled and sliced

Tamarind pulp 2 Tbsp, soaked for 10 minutes in 100 ml (3¹/₃ fl oz / 6 Tbsp) warm water, then strained; reserve tamarind liquid

Preparation

1. Prepare spice paste. Combine all spice paste ingredients except tamarind liquid in a stone mortar or food processor and grind into a fine paste. Add tamarind liquid and grind again until mixture is smooth.

2. Heat oil in a heavy saucepan. Add spice paste and turmeric or pandan leaf and sauté until fragrant.

3. Add coconut milk and bring to a boil.

4. Add eggs and return to a boil. Reduce heat and simmer until sauce is lightly thickened.

5. Season to taste with salt and pepper. Serve hot with rice and a condiment of choice (pages 20–21).

Grilled Aubergines with Spiced Tomato Sauce
Terong Sambal Tomato

Ingredients

Aubergines (eggplants/brinjals) 400 g (14¹/₃ oz), halved lengthwise

Coarse salt 1 Tbsp

Vegetable oil 3 Tbsp

Tomato Sauce

Vegetable oil 2 Tbsp

Shallots 40 g (1¹/₃ oz), peeled and sliced

Garlic 30 g (1 oz), peeled and sliced

Large red chillies 100 g (3¹/₃ oz), halved, seeded and sliced

Bird's eye chillies 5–7, according to taste, sliced

Palm sugar 1 Tbsp

Dried prawn (shrimp) paste (*terasi*) ¹/₂ tsp, roasted

Large red tomatoes 2, about 150 g (5¹/₃ oz), peeled, halved, seeded and diced

Salt to taste

Crushed black pepper to taste

Lime juice 1 Tbsp

Preparation

1. Rub aubergines with salt and vegetable oil. Set aside for 10 minutes.

2. Grill aubergines over moderately hot charcoal or under a grill until they are soft and their skins come off easily. (Alternatively, place aubergines on a wire mesh and grill directly over a gas flame.) Set aside until ready to serve.

3. Prepare sauce. Heat oil in a heavy saucepan. Add shallots and garlic and sauté for 2 minutes until golden. Add chillies and sauté until soft.

4. Add palm sugar and prawn paste and sauté until chillies are caramelised. Stir in tomatoes and sauté until soft, then remove from heat and set aside to cool.

5. Grind sauce coarsely in a stone mortar or food processor. Season to taste with salt, pepper and lime juice.

6. Reheat sauce if necessary and pour over aubergines. Serve hot with rice and condiment of choice (pages 20–21).

Sautéed Cabbage and Green Beans
Gulai Kol dan Bunjis

Ingredients

Vegetable oil 2 Tbsp

Cabbage 300 g (10 oz), cut into 1.5 x 3-cm (³/₄ x 1-in) pieces and blanched

Green beans 300 g (10 oz), cut into 3-cm (1-in) lengths

Large red chillies 50 g (1²/₃ oz), halved, seeded and sliced into fine strips

Salt and pepper to taste

Spice Paste

Shallots 50 g (1²/₃ oz), peeled and sliced

Garlic 30 g (1 oz), peeled and sliced

Ginger 30 g (1 oz), peeled and sliced

Galangal 30 g (1 oz), peeled and sliced

Large red chillies 50 g (1²/₃ oz), seeded and sliced

Sugar 1 tsp

Salt to taste

Crushed black pepper to taste

Preparation

1. Combine all spice paste ingredients in a stone mortar or food processor and grind into a fine paste.

2. Heat oil in a frying pan and sauté spice paste over medium heat until fragrant.

3. Add cabbage and green beans and continue to sauté vegetables, stirring often.

4. When vegetables are almost cooked, add sliced red chilies and toss to mix.

5. Season to taste with salt and pepper.

6. Dish out and serve hot with rice and a condiment of choice (pages 20–21).

The Importance of Rice in Bali

Baas Bali is an old strain of rice that is falling out of favour because of its low-yields, long growing season and susceptibility to insects. However, most Balinese agree that it has the best flavour among the rice strains in Bali.

Baas Bali is a graceful plant that stands as tall as a man, with mature heads that bend over at the top. The grains are short, fat and easy to identify. It is by far the most expensive rice in Bali, costing 50 per cent more than regular rice.

Most of the rice grown in Bali consists of various dwarf varieties, sometimes collectively referred to as "new rice". These dwarf strains are the result of combined efforts put in by The International Rice Research Institute in the Philippines, the Department of Agriculture of Indonesia, and several other organisations to breed strains of high-yield, insect-resistant rice which thrive in short growing seasons. The fact that Indonesia has turned from importing rice to being self-sufficient in the last couple of decades is testimony to the fact that dwarf rice stains have proved very successful.

The colour of most rice is white, but there are also black and red strains found in Bali. They are called *padi injin* (black) and *padi barak* (red). Only the husks are coloured while the grain is white. The colour of the husks however, is water-soluble, so when the rice is cooked, the colour permeates the entire grain.

Padi Injin and padi *barak* are not used in the same way as regular rice, partly because they are expensive and partly because they are glutinous, and become sticky when cooked. For daily meals, the Balinese insist upon having their rice fluffy, with each grain separate, and so these red and black varieties are not suitable. Instead, "sticky rice" as it is popularly called, is used for making cakes, rice wine and for temple offerings. Black rice in particular makes a lovely steamed black rice pudding. Served with coconut milk, it is very popular with tourists and Balinese alike.

Baas Bali is an old strain of rice that is falling out of favour because of its low-yields, long growing season and susceptibility to insects. However, most Balinese agree that it has the best flavour among the rice strains in Bali. It is a graceful plant that stands as tall as a man, with mature heads that bend over at the top. The grains are short, fat and easy to identify. It is by far the most expensive rice in Bali, costing 50 per cent more than regular rice.

Most of the rice grown in Bali consists of various dwarf varieties, sometimes collectively referred to as "new rice". These dwarf strains are the result of combined efforts put in by The International Rice Research Institute in the Philippines, the Department of Agriculture of Indonesia, and several other organisations to breed strains of high-yield, insect-resistant rice which thrive in short growing seasons. The fact that Indonesia has turned from importing rice to being self-sufficient in the last couple of decades is testimony to the fact that dwarf rice stains have proved very successful.

The colour of most rice is white, but there are also black and red strains found in Bali. They are called *padi injin* (black) and *padi barak* (red). Only the husks are coloured while the grain is white. The colour of the husks however, is water-soluble, so when the rice is cooked, the colour permeates the entire grain.

Padi Injin and padi *barak* are not used in the same way as regular rice, partly because they are expensive and partly because they are glutinous, and become sticky when cooked. For daily meals, the Balinese insist upon having their rice fluffy, with each grain separate, and so these red and black varieties are not suitable. Instead, "sticky rice" as it is popularly called, is used for making cakes, rice wine and for temple offerings. Black rice in particular makes a lovely steamed black rice pudding. Served with coconut milk, it is very popular with tourists and Balinese alike.

As for offerings, rice plays a very important role, particularly with its naturally-occurring colours. To the Balinese, the three natural colours of rice symbolise three of the four cardinal directions and the gods that are guardians of these directions. Black is symbolic of Betara Wisnu and the north; white represents Betara Iswara and the east; red is Betara Brahma and the south. Only yellow, the colour of Betara Mahadewa, is missing in rice. But the Balinese make up for this by using turmeric to colour the rice. In presenting the offerings, the different coloured rice are placed facing their symbolic directions, and in the centre is placed a mixture of the four colours, known as *brunbun*, to represent a fifth god, Betara Siwa.

Rice & Noodles

Fried Rice
Nasi Goreng

Although it is not often prepared in private homes, fried rice is a very popular restaurant treat for the Balinese. Each restaurant and cook would have a different way of preparing this dish, but it is commonly cooked using only cold rice and very little oil. You can order it mixed up with almost any kind of meat or vegetables and you may also get a few pieces of fried chicken or some skewers of sate on the side. In Bali, fried rice is often served topped with a fried egg.

Ingredients

Vegetable oil 6 Tbsp

Shallots 6, peeled, halved and sliced

Garlic 6 cloves, peeled and sliced

Carrot 1, peeled and sliced into fine strips

Large red chillies 2, halved, seeded and finely sliced

Bird's eye chillies 2, sliced, optional

White cabbage 100 g (3^1/$_3$ oz), sliced into fine strips

Spiced tomato sauce I or II (page 25) 1 Tbsp

Chicken legs or prawns (shrimps) 200 g (7 oz), dice chicken and peel prawns

Light soy sauce 2 Tbsp

Eggs 2, beaten

Chilled cooked rice 600 g (1 lb 5^1/$_3$ oz)

Celery 30 g (1 oz), sliced

Leek 50 g (1^2/$_3$ oz), sliced

Spinach 50 g (1^2/$_3$ oz), cut into 2.5-cm (1-in) lengths

Salt a pinch

Preparation

1. Heat oil in a heavy frying pan. Add shallots, garlic, carrot and chillies and sauté for 1 minute until shallots and garlic are golden brown.

2. Add cabbage, spiced tomato sauce and chicken and sauté for another 1 minute. Season with soy sauce and sauté until dry.

3. Add eggs and scramble, then add rice. Cook for another 3 minutes then add remaining ingredients except fried shallots. Mix well.

4. Adjust seasoning to taste as necessary. Serve with Spiced Tomato Sauce I (page 25) and fried prawn crackers (page 56), if desired.

Seafood Fried Rice
Nasi Goreng Laut

This recipe makes a terrific dish using leftovers. Just remember not to overcook the rice. Instead, use rice which is slightly under cooked. Spread it on a tray and leave in the refrigerator, uncovered, overnight. This ensures that the rice is very dry when you're ready to cook it. Moist rice will stick to the frying pan and result in a mushy dish!

Ingredients

Vegetable oil 90 ml (3 fl oz / 6 Tbsp)

Shallots 50 g (1²/₃ oz), peeled, halved lengthwise and sliced

Garlic 30 g (1 oz), peeled and sliced

Large red chillies 2, halved, seeded and finely sliced

Bird's eye chillies 2, finely sliced, optional

Prawns (shrimps) 150 g (5¹/₃ oz), peeled and cleaned

Dried anchovies 40 g (1¹/₃ oz), fried, optional

Dried prawn (shrimp) paste (*terasi*) ¹/₂ tsp, roasted, and finely crumbled

Spiced tomato sauce I or II (page 25) 1 Tbsp

Light soy sauce (*kicap asin*) 2 Tbsp

Eggs 2, beaten

Chilled cooked rice 600 g (1 lb 5¹/₃ oz)

Chinese celery leaves 30 g (1 oz), sliced

Spring onions (scallions) 50 g (1²/₃ oz), sliced

Spinach 50 g (1²/₃ oz), sliced

Salt a pinch

Fried shallots (page 23) 2 Tbsp

Preparation

1. Heat oil in a heavy frying pan. Add shallots, garlic and chillies and sauté over medium heat for 1 minute.

2. Add prawns, anchovies and prawn paste and sauté for 30 seconds.

3. Add spiced tomato sauce and soy sauce and continue to fry until dry.

4. Add eggs and continue frying until eggs are scrambled.

5. Add rice and fry for 3 more minutes.

6. Add remaining ingredients, mix well and season to taste.

7. Garnish with fried shallots. Serve with Spiced Tomato Sauce I (page 25) and fried prawn crackers (page 56), if desired.

Chicken Fried Noodles

Mie Goreng Ayam

Ingredients

Vegetable oil 90 ml (3 fl oz / 6 Tbsp)

Boneless chicken leg 160 g (5¹/₃ oz), cut into medium-size cubes

Large red chillies 2, halved, seeded and finely sliced

Bird's eye chillies 2, finely sliced, optional

White cabbage 50 g (1²/₃ oz), finely sliced

Carrots 50 g (1²/₃ oz), peeled and finely sliced into strips

Spiced tomato sauce I or II (page 25) 1 Tbsp

Light soy sauce (*kicap asin*) 2 Tbsp

Eggs 2, beaten

Cooked egg noodles (see Note) 600 g (1 lb 5¹/₃ oz), chilled

Chinese celery leaves 40 g (1¹/₃ oz), sliced

Small leek 60 g (2 oz), sliced

Spring onions (scallions) 80 g (2⁴/₅ oz), sliced

Spinach 80 g (2⁴/₅ oz), sliced

Salt a pinch

Fried shallots (page 23) 2 Tbsp

NOTE

Cook the noodles in rapidly boiling water in a ratio of 100 g (3¹/₃ oz) noodles to 1 litre (32 fl oz / 4 cups) water to which some oil and salt have been added. It should be cooked uncovered until al dente. Drain and use. If you are not using the noodles immediately, rinse the drained noodles in cold water and toss with some vegetable oil to prevent them from sticking.

Preparation

1. Heat oil in a heavy frying pan until smoking hot.
2. Add chicken and sauté over high heat until it changes colour.
3. Add chillies, cabbage and carrots and sauté for 30 seconds. Add spiced tomato sauce and soy sauce, and fry again for 1 minute.
4. Add eggs and continue frying until eggs are scrambled.
5. Add noodles and fry for 3 more minutes, tossing and stirring continuously.
6. Add remaining ingredients, mix well and season to taste.
7. Dish out and serve with Spiced Tomato Sauce I (page 25), if desired.

The Chinese Soup Connection

When watching the preparation of soup dishes in Bali, you may be taken by how closely they resemble Chinese soups. The influence of Chinese cooking is clear, and the resultant dish is similar to those found in food courts and kitchens throughout South East Asia, in particular the Chinese and Malay soup dishes sold by hawkers in Singapore. Here in Bali, soups can be divided into two major categories—*sop* and *soto*.

Sops

These are mostly clear soups made with chicken, beef or fish stock, served with an array of garnishes such as meatballs, fishballs—often the size of ping pong balls and advertised as *bakso tennis*—deep-fried bean curd and vegetables like Chinese bok choi, Chinese cabbage, bean sprouts, celery and leeks. Two types of noodles are most often used, translucent glass noodles and egg noodles. The dishes are usually assembled only when a customer makes an order.

First, the noodles are blanched briefly in boiling stock, then placed in a soup bowl. Next, the sliced vegetables are quickly blanched and place on top of the noodles, followed by meatballs and bean curd. Finally, the hot soup is ladled over. To finish off the dish, most vendors would add a 'secret topping' which makes their soup distinct from the competition. This is served with a fiery dip of freshly sliced bird's eye chillies and wedges of lime as well as a selection of other commercially manufactured sauces.

Some of the most popular *sops* are *baksos* (meatball soups), and the ever popular *sop ayam* (chicken noodle soup).

Soto

*Soto*s are creamy, meat stews enriched with coconut milk, a little like Malaysian *laksa*. There are various *soto*s, including *soto babad* which is made from cow's stomach, *gule,* which originated from Java, and is usually made with goat meat. (As goats are not raised by the Balinese people, it is likely that any dish containing goat meat comes from Java.)

The rich meat *soto*s from Java and Sumatra are often oily and served dry with very little sauce. Tough cuts of beef or goat are cooked for hours in a coconut-based stock, resulting in very tasty meat soups that are eaten as full meals. Most popular are the *gule*s found in various *warung*s on the way to the airport near Kuta.

Beef Dumpling Noodle Soup *Bakso Sapi*

Ingredients

Asian egg noodles 120 g (4 oz), cooked
Firm bean curd 120 g (4 oz), sliced and deep-fried
Wonton wrappers 8

Stock

Chicken carcass 3 kg (6 lb 9 oz), fat and skin removed, chopped
Beef bones or trimmings 3 kg (6 lb 9 oz), chopped
Vegetable oil 3 Tbsp
Shallots 200 g (7 oz), peeled and sliced
Garlic 100 g (3¹/₃ oz), peeled and sliced
Leeks 75 g (2²/₃ oz), just the white parts, sliced
Celery stalks 75 g (2²/₃ oz), sliced
Large red chillies 3
Bird's eye chillies 5–7, according to taste, bruised
Lemongrass 4 stalks, ends trimmed, bruised
Salam **leaves** 5
Kaffir lime leaves 5, bruised
Coriander seeds 2 Tbsp, toasted and crushed
Crushed black pepper 2 Tbsp
Cloves 8, crushed
Salt to taste

Beef Dumplings

Beef topside 150 g (5¹/₃ oz), minced
Spring onions (scallions) 10 g (¹/₃ oz), sliced
Oyster sauce 1 Tbsp
Sweet soy sauce (*kicap manis*) 1 tsp
Light soy sauce (*kicap asin*) 1 tsp
Potato flour 1 Tbsp
Ground white pepper a pinch
Salt a pinch
Ground nutmeg a pinch

Preparation

1. Prepare stock. Rinse chicken and beef bones until water runs clear. Place in a stockpot and fill with enough cold water to cover bones. Bring to boil over high heat.

2. Drain and discard water. Wash bones again under running water and return bones to a larger stockpot, adding 3 times as much water. Bring to a boil again. Reduce heat and skim away scum as it rises to the surface.

3. In a separate saucepan, heat oil and sauté shallots and garlic over medium heat for 2 minutes. Add leeks, celery, chillies, lemongrass and *salam* leaves. Continue to sauté for 2 minutes. Add 500 ml (16 fl oz / 2 cups) water and all remaining stock ingredients, and return to the boil. Add this to the stockpot containing beef bones and chicken carcass.

4. Let it simmer for 5–6 hours over very low heat. Skim off scum often. When done, strain stock.

5. Prepare beef dumplings. Combine all dumpling ingredients in a bowl and mix into a smooth paste. Season to taste. Divide paste into 2 equal portions.

6. Use one portion to make wontons. Place 1 tsp beef filling in the centre of a wanton wrapper and fold sides up into the shape of a cup. Seal edges of wrapper with some egg white or water. Repeat with wonton wrappers until this portion of beef filling is used up.

7. To cook wontons, place 4 wontons into the simmering chicken stock and poach for 3 minutes. Repeat with remaining 4 wontons. (Alternatively, steam them for 3 minutes.)

8. Once done, deep-fry cooked wontons in medium hot oil until crispy. Drain on paper towels.

9. Make beef balls with remaining paste. Using 2 tablespoons, shape spoonsful of minced meat mixture into balls. Slide them into the simmering stock and poach for 2 minutes and set aside.

10. Serve noodles in individual portions. Bring stock to a boil. Divide heated wontons, dumplings, noodles and bean curd into 4 large soup bowls and ladle over with boiling stock.

11. Garnish with sliced Chinese celery leaves and fried shallots.

12. Serve with tomato ketchup and sweet soy sauce on the side, if desired.

Chicken Noodle Soup
Soto Ayam

Ingredients

Chicken 1, about 1.2 kg (2 lb 10 oz)

Chicken stock (page 23) 2.5 litres (80 fl oz / 10 cups)

Glass noodles 100 g (3¹/₃ oz), soaked in warm water to soften

Hard-boiled eggs 4, peeled and cut into wedges

Chinese celery leaves 50 g (1²/₃ oz), shredded

Bean sprouts 50 g (1²/₃ oz), blanched for 15 seconds, then drained and cooled

Fried shallots (page 23) 2 Tbsp

Vegetable oil 2 Tbsp

Spice Paste

Shallots 80 g (2⁴/₅ oz), peeled and sliced

Garlic 50 g (1²/₃ oz), peeled and sliced

Ginger 30 g (1 oz), peeled and sliced

Galangal 30 g (1 oz), peeled and sliced

Turmeric 30 g (1 oz), peeled and sliced

Candlenuts 20 g (²/₃ oz), roasted and crushed

Bird's eye chillies 3, sliced

Crushed black pepper ¹/₂ tsp

Cloves 5, crushed

Cinnamon stick 10-cm (4-in) length

Sweet soy sauce (*kicap manis*) 4 Tbsp

Lemongrass 2, ends trimmed, bruised

Kaffir lime leaves 3, bruised

Preparation

1. Prepare spice paste. Combine all ingredients in a stone mortar or food processor and grind coarsely.

2. Heat oil in a soup pot. Add spice paste and sauté until fragrant.

3. Strain chicken stock into fragrant spice paste. Bring to a boil and let it simmer for 15 minutes. Season to taste with salt and pepper.

4. Wash chicken thoroughly and place in stock. Reduce heat and simmer until chicken is very tender. Takes about 1 hour. Turn off heat and allow chicken to cool in stock.

5. When cool enough to handle, remove chicken from stock and shred meat finely by hand.

6. Briefly blanch glass noodles, then plunge in iced water to stop the cooking process. Drain.

7. Just before serving, return chicken stock to a simmer. Blanch noodles in stock briefly to heat through and place in individual serving bowls.

8. Place single portions of shredded chicken, bean sprouts and celery leaves in a deep sieve and lower into simmering chicken stock for 1 minute to heat through. Place over glass noodles. Ladle over hot chicken stock. Garnish with fried shallots and hard-boiled egg. Serve immediately.

Chicken Porridge
Bubur Ayam Masak Bali

Ingredients

Porridge

Chicken stock (page 23) 1.5 litres (48 fl oz / 6 cups)
Chicken 1, about 1.2 kg (2 lb 10 oz)
Vegetable oil 2 Tbsp
Shallots 50 g (1^2/$_3$ oz), peeled and sliced
Garlic 30 g (1 oz), peeled and sliced
Salam **leaves** 3
Lemongrass 1 stalk, ends trimmed, bruised
Long-grain rice 300 g (10 oz), washed and rinsed
Salt to taste
Crushed black pepper a pinch
Fried shallots (page 23) 2 Tbsp

Salad Vegetables

Corn kernels 100 g (3^1/$_3$ oz), blanched
Long beans 100 g (3^1/$_3$ oz), cut into 3-cm (1^1/$_4$-in) lengths, blanched
Bean sprouts 100 g (3^1/$_3$ oz), blanched
Large red chillies 2, seeded and sliced
Grated coconut 250 g (9 oz), lightly roasted

Salad Dressing

Vegetable oil 2 Tbsp
Fried shallots (page 23) 3 Tbsp
Fried garlic (page 23) 1 Tbsp
Bird's eye chillies 1 Tbsp, sliced and fried
Dried prawn (shrimp) paste (*terasi*) ^{1}/$_2$ tsp, roasted
Kaffir lime leaves 3, finely chopped
Salt to taste
Crushed black pepper a pinch
Palm sugar 1 Tbsp, chopped
Lesser galangal (*kencur*) 1 Tbsp, washed and finely grounded

Spice Paste

Large red chillies 4, halved, seeded and sliced
Bird's eye chillies 3–4, sliced
Shallots 30 g (1 oz), peeled and sliced
Garlic 30 g (1 oz), peeled and sliced
Galangal 30 g (1 oz), peeled and thinly sliced
Turmeric 30 g (1 oz), peeled and sliced
Lesser galangal (*kencur*) 20 g (^{2}/$_3$ oz), washed, sliced
Candlenuts 40 g (1^1/$_3$ oz)
Coriander seeds ^{1}/$_2$ tsp, crushed
Crushed white pepper a pinch
Dried prawn (shrimp) paste (*terasi*) ^{1}/$_4$ tsp, roasted and crumbled
Salt a pinch
Salam **leaves** 1
Lemongrass 1 stalk, ends trimmed, bruised
Vegetable oil 2 Tbsp

Chayote

Chayote (*joko*) 2, medium-size, sliced into even strips and blanched
Chicken stock (page 23) 125 ml (4 fl oz / ^{1}/$_2$ cup)
Coconut milk 125 ml (4 fl oz / ^{1}/$_2$ cup)
Salt a pinch
Crushed white pepper ^{1}/$_4$ tsp

Coconut Sambal

Grated coconut ^{2}/$_3$ cup, freshly grated
Lime juice 1 tsp

Garnish

Fried shallots (page 23) 2 Tbsp
Fried soy beans or peanuts 2 Tbsp

Preparation

1. Prepare chicken stock. Simmer it for 4 hours.

2. Add whole chicken and simmer for 1 hour or until chicken meat is very tender and falls off the bones.

3. Remove chicken from stock and place in a deep bowl. Strain stock through a fine sieve into the bowl. Leave chicken to cool in stock.

4. When cool enough to handle, remove chicken from stock and shred meat by hand. Set shredded meat aside.

5. Prepare porridge. Heat oil in a heavy saucepan. Add shallots, garlic, *salam* leaves and lemongrass and sauté for 2 minutes over medium heat.

6. Add rice and sauté for 1 minute.

7. Add half the chicken stock and bring to boil. Lower heat and simmer until rice is very soft but not overcooked. While simmering, add more stock as liquid evaporates.

8. Mix in half the shredded chicken, then season to taste with salt and pepper.

9. Prepare dressing for salad. Combine all dressing ingredients and blend well. Place salad vegetables in a large bowl and toss with dressing. Garnish with fried shallots and set aside.

10. Prepare spice paste and chayote. Combine all spice paste ingredients, except oil, in a stone mortar or food processor and grind into a fine paste.

11. Heat oil in a heavy saucepan and sauté ground spices for a few minutes until fragrant. Transfer one-third of spice paste to a dish and set aside for coconut sambal.

12. Meanwhile, add blanched chayote into the saucepan and sauté for 2 minutes over medium heat.

13. Add vegetable or chicken stock and coconut milk, bring to boil, then reduce heat and simmer until sauce lightly thickens. Season to taste with salt and pepper. Set aside.

14. Prepare coconut sambal. In a saucepan, heat reserved spice paste and add grated coconut. Sauté for 2 minutes. If sambal becomes a little too dry, stir in small amounts of water or chicken stock. Adjust to taste with lime juice. Set aside and cool to room temperature.

15. When cool, place in a stone mortar and grind into a fine, oily sauce.

16. To serve, divide porridge into 4 bowls. Spoon 1 Tbsp coconut sambal evenly over porridge and top with a generous spoonful of salad and chayote. Garnish with fried shallots and soy beans or peanuts. Serve immediately.

NOTE

Chayote can be substituted with green papaya, cucumber, celery, carrot, green beans and snake beans. Green papaya, cucumber and celery do not require blanching.

Jimbaran Seafood Cafés

Fish is a major source of food for most Balinese. The staple protein for all who live on or near the sea, fish is relatively cheap, not too difficult to catch and easily available in the markets. Fishing has been one of the principal occupations for many villagers living in the small fishing village of Jimbaran just south of the airport, up till the advent of mass tourism into the area which transformed once-quiet beaches like Jimbaran Beach into a tourist heaven with international hotels and innumerable seafood restaurants moving in.

When this happened in the early 1990s, a few creative local fishermen set up simple barbecues along the stretch of beach and began to grill their freshly caught fish for the ever-hungry tourist hoards. With their success, more operators gradually moved in and opened even more sophisticated seafood grills and restaurants.

Over the years, local community boards started to take control of these developments, resulting in three clusters where visitors can enjoy sometimes-spectacular sunsets while sipping on a cool Bintang beer and feasting on a sumptuous seafood dinner. Perhaps the smartest restaurants today are located at the northern end of the Jimbaran Beach (near the Four Seasons Resort) which offers organised parking, adequate security, toilets and relatively high sanitation standards.

It is common knowledge that almost all of these restaurants pay lucrative commissions—as high as 40 per cent of your total bill—to any guide or taxi driver who brings guests to the restaurants for a meal. (Indeed, you won't be surprised to find that your taxi driver or guide has a family member or friend running one of these restaurants!) As such, their recommendations may not be based on the merit of these eating establishments but on the commission they are likely to get. So if you come to Bali with the address of a restaurant a friend had recommended based on his experience there, stick firmly to it and do not let the taxi driver direct you to his "personal favourite", nor believe him if he insists that restaurant had just closed down the week before!

Seafood

Grilled Mackerel in Banana Leaf
Tambusan Be Pasih

This recipe originates from Amed, a small fishing town northeast of Bali. Here, Pak Nyoman usually sets off from his family home well before sunrise for his daily fishing venture, and returns home 3 hours later with a respectable catch of mackerels and small tuna. Putu, his wife, then takes over, cleaning, marinating and wrapping the fish. This is always done in front of their house in their little *bale* (pavilion) along the main road which leads to the dive resorts in the north eastern corner of Bali.

Once Putu is done, Pak Nyoman grills the fish and starts his business day. Customers often buy a couple of the fish from him to take away or to eat on the spot. It is often served over a generous helping of rice, together with condiments of spiced tomato sauce, raw cucumbers, long beans and lemon basil.

Ingredients

Mackerel fillet 600 g (1 lb 5 oz), skinned, boned and cut into 1.5-cm (³/₄-in) cubes

Salt a pinch

Crushed black pepper a pinch

Spice paste for seafood (page 26) 125 g (4¹/₂ oz)

Salam **leaves** 4

Banana leaves 4, cut into 15-cm (6-in) squares

Tomatoes 2, quartered

Lemon basil 8 sprigs

Bamboo skewers or cocktail sticks

NOTE

Do not overcook these delicate parcels as the fish tends to dry out quickly. Instead, under cook them slightly, then let them rest in a warm place for 5 minutes. If banana leaves are not available, corn husks can be used as a substitute.

Preparation

1. Season fish with salt and pepper, then mix with spice paste.

2. Place 1 *salam* leaf onto the centre of a banana leaf. Top with 1 Tbsp marinated fish, 2 tomato wedges and 2 sprigs lemon basil.

3. Fold one-third of banana leaf over ingredients and roll up tightly. Secure ends with skewers or cocktail sticks. Repeat until ingredients are used up.

4. Cover parcels and leave to marinate in a cool place for 30 minutes.

5. Parcels can be cooked in a few ways—steamed over rapidly boiling water for 7 minutes, grilled over very low heat for 9 minutes or baked in an oven preheated to 180°C (350°F) for 9 minutes.

6. Alternatively, steam for 4 minutes, then place over charcoal heat or under a grill and cook for 3 minutes until banana leaves are evenly browned.

7. Perhaps the most common way in Bali is to place the parcels on a dry, heated iron plate or a frying pan and cook until done.

8. It is important that the parcels are not overcooked because the fish dries out very quickly. Instead, undercook them slightly, then leave them to rest in a warm place for 5 minutes to cook in the residual heat.

9. Serve with shallot and lemon grass dressing (page 20), if desired.

A Word About Fresh Fish

Coming to a balmy island, most visitors expect to find the freshest seafood available in large quantities here. Sadly, that is not altogether true. With the influx of large-scale tourism and the rapid increase of the island's population, the ever-growing demand for high quality seafood has placed a devastating strain on the environment. Where in the past, fishermen only needed to catch enough fish to feed his family, there is today an insatiable demand for an ever-diminishing supply of seafood. Coupled with the lack of fishing restrictions and quotas, it is common to see fishermen hauling in empty fishing nets in the early morning hours and undersized fishes and crustaceans being sold in the fish market in Kedonganan. In fact, while you will see baskets of small tunas, bonitos, flying fish, mackerels, sardines and colourful parrot fish in the markets, the fish available to the local community are those of secondary quality, caught not from the waters off Bali but trucked in less-than-ideal conditions from East Java.

You will often see displays of seafood in restaurants in Bali. As part of the experience, most operators will ask you to choose your own fish while assuring you how fresh their seafood is. Rather than take their word for it, know how to recognise a fresh specimen when you see one.

Most of the restaurant operators will open the gills and show you how strikingly red they are. This can be rather misleading as there are several ways to keep gills red for longer period of times, often with the help of suspicious substances. If you are not familiar with the specific type of fish, then it is impossible to tell by the look of the gills whether the fish is fresh. What is more reliable is to select the fish by the look of its eyes: they must be bright and crystal clear, sticking out from the eye socket in the shape of a half moon. The flesh must be firm to the touch and the skin shiny and slippery, scales should be firmly attached to the skin, and the fish should smell clean and fresh like the ocean. They should also be displayed generously covered with ice, and not in open baskets or boxes. For crustaceans and shellfish, select only live ones as dead shellfish could pose a severe health risk when consumed. Keep an eye on the weighing scale too, as there are countless stories of how scales are adjusted and 'pre-tipped' to be on the heavy side.

Marinated Grilled Fish
Ikan Bakar

Ingredients

Assorted fish fillets 1 kg (2 lb 3 oz)

Salt 1 tsp

Crushed black pepper 1 tsp

Lime juice 2 Tbsp

Spice paste for seafood (page 26) 200 g (7 oz)

Marinade

Large red chillies 150 g (5$^1/_3$ oz), halved, seeded and sliced

Garlic 30 g (1 oz), peeled and sliced

Shallots 80 g (2$^2/_3$ oz), peeled and sliced

Turmeric 60 g (2 oz), peeled and sliced

Ginger 30 g (1 oz), peeled and sliced

Candlenuts 40 g (1$^1/_3$ oz)

Tomatoes 70 g (2$^1/_3$ oz), halved and sliced

Coriander seeds 1 tsp

Dried prawn (shrimp) paste (*terasi*) 1 tsp, roasted

Salt 1 tsp

Vegetable oil 2 Tbsp

Tamarind pulp 1 Tbsp, seeds and fibre removed

***Salam* leaf** 1

Lemongrass 1, ends trimmed, bruised

Water 70 ml (2$^1/_3$ fl oz / $^1/_4$ cup)

NOTE

As a variation to this recipe, a whole fish such as snapper, trevally or mackerel, or assorted seafood such as prawns, clams and mussels can be used in place of fish fillets.

Preparation

1. Prepare marinade. Combine all ingredients except oil, tamarind pulp, *salam* leaves, lemongrass and water in a stone mortar or food processor and grind into a fine paste.

2. Heat oil in a heavy saucepan. Add paste and remaining marinade ingredients and simmer over medium heat until liquid has evaporated and sauce is fragrant. Leave to cool. Set aside one-quarter of marinade for a basting mix and season fish with remaining marinade.

3. Marinate fish with salt, pepper, lime juice and spice paste for seafood. Set aside. If using whole fish, cut fish in half to butterfly, starting from the head down towards the tail along the back bone, then cut 4 slits about 1-cm ($^1/_2$-in) deep on the opposite side of bones. Season fish with salt, pepper, lime juice and spice paste for seafood. If using assorted seafood, season with salt, pepper, lime juice and spice paste for seafood.

4. Prepare basting mix. Combine reserved marinade with an equal amount of vegetable oil. Brush some of this marinade evenly over fish.

5. Grill fish over medium heat. Turn frequently and brush with basting mix until done.

6. Serve with shallot and lemongrass dressing (page 20) if desired.

Minced Fish Grilled in Banana Leaf *Pesan be Pasih*

Ingredients

Fish fillet 600 g (1 lb 5$\frac{1}{3}$ oz), skinned and cut into 1.5-cm ($\frac{3}{4}$-in) cubes

Salt a pinch

Crushed white pepper $\frac{1}{4}$ tsp

Spice paste for seafood (page 26) 125 g (4$\frac{1}{2}$ oz)

Tomatoes 2, each cut into 14 thin slices

Lemon basil 2 sprigs

Salam **leaves** 14

Banana leaves 8, each cut into two 15-cm (6in) squares

Toothpicks as needed

Preparation

1. Season fish with salt and pepper, then coat evenly with spice paste.

2. Place a *salam* leaf in the centre of a banana leaf, then top with 1 heaped tablespoonful of fish, 2 slices tomatoes and lemon basil leaves.

3. Fold long edges of banana leaf in towards each other to enclose filling, then secure open ends with toothpicks. Continue until ingredients are used up.

4. Leave parcels in a cool place for 30 minutes for fish to marinate before cooking.

5. The most common way to cook these parcels is to place them on to a hot iron plate or steel frying pan without oil and grill until done. Alternatively, you can:

   a. Steam them for 7 minutes

   b. Steam them for 4 minutes, then place on a charcoal flame or under a grill and cook for 3 more minutes until banana leaves are evenly browned

   c. Grill them over very low heat for about 9 minutes

Fried Catfish in Turmeric & Tamarind Sauce
Ikan Lele Goreng

Ingredients

Catfish 4, each about 350 g (12 oz)

Salt 1 tsp

Crushed black pepper 1 tsp

Lime juice 4 Tbsp

Vegetable oil for deep-frying

Tamarind pulp 1 Tbsp, seeds and fibre removed

Sour starfruit 2, sliced

Lemongrass 2 stalks, ends trimmed, bruised

Salam **leaves** 2

Chicken stock (page 23) 125 ml (4 fl oz / ½ cup)

Coconut milk 250 ml (8 fl oz / 1 cup)

Sauce

Large red chillies 125 g (4½ oz), halved, seeded and sliced

Shallots 60 g (2 oz), peeled and sliced

Garlic 20 g (⅔ oz), peeled and sliced

Ginger 30 g (1 oz), peeled and sliced

Turmeric 50 g (1⅔ oz), peeled and sliced

Candlenuts 30 g (1 oz)

Dried prawn (shrimp) paste (*terasi*) 1 tsp, roasted

Coriander seeds 1 tsp, roasted and crushed

Tomatoes 50 g (1⅔ oz), halved seeded and sliced

Vegetable oil 3 Tbsp

Preparation

1. Clean fish inside and out. Cut into 75 g (2⅔ oz) pieces or cut into fillets and slice each fillet into 3 portions.
2. Season with salt, pepper and lime juice. Leave to marinate for 30 minutes.
3. Heat oil and deep-fry fish over low heat until crispy, then set aside on a paper towel.
4. Prepare sauce. Combine sauce ingredients, except oil, in a stone mortar or food processor and grind into a fine paste.
5. Heat oil in a heavy saucepan and sauté paste for a few minutes until fragrant.
6. Add tamarind pulp, starfruit, lemongrass and *salam* leaves and sauté for another minute.
7. Add stock and bring to a boil. Lower heat and let it simmer until most of the liquid has evaporated.
8. Stir in coconut milk and return to a boil. Reduce heat and simmer over low heat for 10 minutes until coconut milk breaks and sauce becomes oily and clear rather than creamy.
9. Add fried fish to sauce and mix well. Season to taste with salt, pepper and a generous squeeze of lime juice.

Marinated Mahi Mahi Steamed in Bamboo
Timbungan

Ingredients

Mahi mahi fillet 600 g (1 lb 5 $^1/_3$ oz), skinned, cleaned and diced

Spice paste for seafood (page 26) 125 g (4$^1/_2$ oz)

Lime juice 1 Tbsp

Salt a pinch

Ground black pepper a pinch

Grated coconut 100 g (3$^1/_3$ oz)

Coconut milk 125 ml (4 fl oz / $^1/_2$ cup)

Fried shallots (page 23) 2 Tbsp

Fried garlic (page 23) 2 Tbsp

Bird's eye chillies 2, finely chopped

Palm sugar 1 tsp, chopped

Kaffir lime leaves $^1/_2$ tsp, finely chopped

Salam **leaf** 1

Tomatoes 2, halved and sliced

Lemon basil 8 sprigs

Small section of bamboo (see Note) 1, cut open

NOTE

Use snapper or mackerel if mahi mahi is not available. The Balinese also often use eel and crab, and sometimes also prawns for this dish.

To prepare the bamboo, cut it into half lengthwise. Scrub the bamboo clean and steam for 30 minutes. If bamboo is not available, use banana leaves or corn husks.

Preparation

1. Combine fish, spice paste, lime juice, salt and pepper. Mix well and leave to marinate in the refrigerator for 10 minutes.

2. Add grated coconut, coconut milk, fried shallots and garlic, chillies, palm sugar and kaffir lime leaves and mix well.

3. Place a *salam* leaf in the bottom of a bamboo section, then layer it with fish mixture, tomato and basil until the bamboo is fully packed.

4. Cover with the other half of bamboo and steam for about 15 minutes. Alternatively, place the filled bamboo on hot charcoal and bake for 10 minutes. Serve.

Prawns in Banana Leaf
Tum Udang

Ingredients

Prawns (shrimps) 600 g (1 lb 5¹⁄₃ oz), peeled and deveined

Grated coconut 120 g (4 oz)

Fried garlic (page 23) 3 Tbsp

Fried shallots (page 23) 3 Tbsp

Bird's eye chillies 2–4, according to taste, sliced and fried

Kaffir lime leaves 2, finely chopped

Salam **leaves** 12

Banana leaf squares 12, each 15 x 15-cm (6 x 6-in)

Banana leaf strips 12, each 2.5 x 15 cm (1 x 6-in)

Bamboo skewers 12

Spice Paste

Large red chillies 100 g (3¹⁄₃ oz), halved, seeded and sliced

Bird's eye chillies 3–5, according to taste, sliced

Garlic 30 g (1 oz), peeled and sliced

Shallots 80 g (2⁴⁄₅ oz), peeled and sliced

Turmeric 60 g (2 oz), peeled and sliced

Ginger 30 g (1 oz), peeled and sliced

Candlenuts 40 g (1¹⁄₃ oz)

Tomatoes 70 g (2¹⁄₃ oz), halved and seeded

Coriander seeds 1 tsp

Dried prawn (shrimp) paste (*terasi*) 1 tsp, roasted

Vegetable oil 2 Tbsp

Tamarind pulp 1 Tbsp, seeds and fibre removed

Salam **leaf** 1

Lemongrass 1 stalk, ends trimmed, bruised

Preparation

1. Combine all spice paste ingredients, except the oil, tamarind pulp, *salam* leaf and lemongrass in a mortar or food processor and grind into a fine paste.

2. Heat oil in a heavy saucepan and add paste and remaining spice paste ingredients and simmer over medium heat until all the liquid has evaporated and spice paste is fragrant and glossy. Set aside to cool before using.

3. Spoon 180 ml (6 fl oz / ³⁄₄ cup) of the prepared spice paste into a mixing bowl and add prawns, grated coconut, fried garlic and shallots, chillies and kaffir lime leaves. Mix well.

4. Place 1 *salam* leaf in the centre of a banana leaf. Spoon 1 Tbsp grated coconut mixture onto the *salam* leaf and fold the banana leaf to enclose the mixture, forming a little purse. Wrap over with one extra strip of banana leaf and secure with a bamboo skewer.

5. Steam parcels for 7–10 minutes.

6. Serve with steamed rice, vegetables and Spiced Tomato Sauce I or II (page 25), if desired.

Snacking—
A Way of Life

For almost all Balinese, eating at home is only half the picture. The Balinese love eating snacks. Little food stalls called *warung* are found in every village neighborhood which serve as both a food store and as a social center. This is where people come to swap stories, catch up on the local gossip and where a family can bring a marriageable daughter to the public eye.

Many kinds of *warung* abound all over Bali. Some serve full meals, usually in the form of *nasi bungkus,* steamed rice mixed with side dishes wrapped in a banana leaf, while others sell sate. This is the sort of 'restaurant' to which the average Balinese will go for a full meal if he was unable to eat at home. The cost of all one can eat is not more then US$0.75 to US$1. But most *warung* just serve cakes, coffee, local fruit and a large assortment of sweet and salty snacks, from peanuts to commercially packaged treats. And they are immensely popular with Balinese of all ages.

Then there are the push-carts. If you wait long enough, sooner or later one will come by your front door. Each cart specialises in one kind of food. Some sell *kacang ijo* (green pea porridge), while others sell *rujak* (spicy, sour, sweet vegetable fruit salad), corn on the cob, drinks, and peanuts.

Then there are the temporary *warungs* which, no matter how small, are always set up at religious festivals. There is never any need to bring your own food because you can be sure that every imaginable kind of food will be hawked on the spot.

With so much ready food to be found, it is no wonder that snacking is an institution in most parts of Bali. It is estimated that perhaps 30 per cent of the average Balinese's food intake consists of food consumed outside regular meal times.

A casual trip trough any Balinese village reveals the truth of snacking. Wherever Balinese people gather to sit and chat, test their fighting cocks, perform their obligatory group work functions, have *banjar* meetings, wash bodies, pray or celebrate, you will find snack sellers and eager customers. However, during the hottest times of the day, a visit to almost any house compound will reveal kids munching on something or other. Snack sellers even penetrate the inner sanctums of offices. Once when visiting the Governor's office, a snack vendor walked in, took his metal box from his head and all business stopped briefly as the office staff made their snack selections!

Light Bites

Savoury Lamb Pancakes
Murtabak

Ingredients

Vegetable oil 2 Tbsp

Garlic 20 g ($^2/_3$ oz), peeled and sliced

Lean beef 300 g (10 oz), minced

Lamb shoulder 300 g (10 oz), minced

Onion 50 g (1$^2/_3$ oz), peeled and sliced

Small leek 30 g (1 oz), cleaned, halved and sliced

Large red chilli 1, halved, seeded and sliced

Chinese celery leaves or coriander (cilantro) leaves
10 g ($^1/_3$ oz), chopped

Curry powder 1 Tbsp

Eggs 4

Spring onions (scallions) 20 g ($^2/_3$ oz), sliced

Salt to taste

Ground white pepper to taste

Dough

Plain all-purpose flour 250 g (2 lb,1$^2/_3$ oz)

Vegetable oil 3 Tbsp

Water 180 ml (6 fl oz / $^3/_4$ cup)

Salt a pinch

Preparation

1. Prepare dough. Combine all ingredients and knead into an oily, elastic dough. Cover and leave to rest at room temperature for 2 hours.

2. Divide dough into 4 portions and roll each portion into a ball. Flatten dough on an oily surface (preferably marble) and pull it into a square, thin sheet about 30 x 30-cm (12 x 12-in).

3. Prepare filling. Heat 2 Tbsp vegetable oil in a heavy saucepan. Add garlic and sauté over medium heat for 1 minute.

4. Add minced beef and lamb, increase heat and continue to sauté until meats change colour.

5. Add onion, leek, chilli and celery or coriander leaves and continue to sauté for another minute.

6. Mix in curry powder and sauté for another minute. Set side to cool.

7. Place meat mixture in a deep bowl, mix in eggs and spring onions, and season to taste with salt and pepper.

8. To assemble pancakes, heat a generous amount of oil in a heavy frying pan or griddle. Place a sheet of dough in the centre and spoon one-quarter of filling into the middle of dough sheet.

9. Fold sides of dough towards the centre to enclose filling. Leave to cook for 2 minutes, then flip the pancake over and fry until pancake turns golden brown and crispy. While frying, baste often with hot oil.

10. Repeat with rest of ingredients.

11. When done, cut pancakes into even pieces. In Bali, these pancakes are served with pickled vegetables, whole green bird's eye chillies and a light curry sauce.

Sweet Corn Pancakes
Bergedel Jagung

Ingredients

Sweet corn kernels 600 g (1 lb 5$^1/_3$ oz)

Plain (all-purpose) flour 2 Tbsp

Egg 1

Chinese celery leaves 2 Tbsp, roughly chopped

Salt to taste

Crushed white pepper a pinch

Vegetable oil for deep-frying

Vegetable Spice Paste

Large red chillies 50 g (1$^2/_3$ oz), halved, seeded and sliced

Bird's eye chillies 2–3, finely sliced

Shallots 20 g ($^2/_3$ oz), peeled and sliced

Garlic 20 g ($^2/_3$ oz), peeled and sliced

Turmeric 20 g ($^2/_3$ oz), peeled and sliced

Galangal 20 g ($^2/_3$ oz), peeled and sliced

Candlenuts 20 g ($^2/_3$ oz), peeled and sliced

Coriander seeds $^1/_2$ tsp

Ground white pepper $^1/_4$ tsp

Dried prawn (shrimp) paste (*terasi*) $^1/_2$ tsp, roasted

Salt $^1/_2$ tsp

Vegetable oil 3 Tbsp

Preparation

1. Prepare spice paste. Combine all spice paste ingredients, except oil, in a stone mortar or food processor and grind coarsely into a paste.

2. Heat oil in a heavy saucepan and sauté paste over medium heat until fragrant. Remove and set aside to cool before using.

3. Place corn kernels in a stone mortar and grind coarsely.

4. Add vegetable spice paste, flour, egg, celery leaves, salt and pepper and continue to grind into a smooth paste.

5. Using a tablespoon, form the corn mixture into even-size patties.

6. Heat oil for deep-frying over medium heat. Lower patties into hot oil and deep-fry until golden. Do this in batches.

7. Drain patties well on paper towels.

8. Serve warm with a condiment of choice (pages 20–21).

ESSENTIAL TIPS ON DEEP-FRYING

To get the most out of deep-frying, use only heat-resistant, non-foaming fat. Peanut oil, safflower oil, sunflower oil and canola oil are ideal. Deep-fry at a temperature between 160°C (325°F) and 180°C (350°F). Avoid lowering the heat as this will open the pores of the food being fried, causing the food to absorb the oil and become soggy. Rising heat closes the pores and guarantees a light, crisp result. After each use, remember to filter the oil.

Jagung

Corn or *jagung* as it is called in Bali, is the most popular cooked vegetable snack here, enjoyed either steamed (*jagung malablab*) or roasted over open coals (*jagung matunu* or *jagung panggang*).

It is easy to find push-cart hawkers selling corn wherever there is a crowd. The big open-air market at Candi Kuning south of Bedugul is famous for its boiled corn because it is the source of the freshest corn in Bali. You will also find roast corn sold along the black sand beach just north of the Hotel Bali Beach in Sanur, or along Jimbaran in the late afternoons and evenings.

Each push-cart has a little charcoal fire over which the fresh corn is grilled, as well as a steam pan built in, around which the corn is neatly arranged. In the centre is yet another snack—freshly steamed peanuts. The choice is then up to you whether you prefer sweet juicy steamed corn, or corn grilled over glowing charcoal. To enhance the flavour, margarine is often brushed onto the corn.

Fried Vegetable Patties
Sayur Goreng Gorengan

Ingredients

Carrots 100 g (3^1/$_3$ oz), peeled and sliced
Bean sprouts 100 g (3^1/$_3$ oz), cleaned
Spring onions (scallions) 100 g (3^1/$_3$ oz), sliced
Leeks 100 g (3^1/$_3$ oz), sliced into fine strips
Vegetable oil for deep-frying

Marinade

Vegetable oil 2 Tbsp
Garlic 20 g (^{2}/$_3$ oz), peeled and sliced
Shallots 30 g (1 oz), peeled and sliced
Turmeric 20 g (^{2}/$_3$ oz), peeled and sliced
Ginger 20 g (^{2}/$_3$ oz), peeled and sliced
Bird's eye chillies 2-4
Candlenuts 20 g (^{2}/$_3$ oz), roasted
Coriander seeds 1 Tbsp, roasted
Crushed white pepper ^{1}/$_4$ tsp

Batter

Cake flour 125 g (4^1/$_2$ oz)
Rice flour 50 g (1^2/$_3$ oz)
Water 125 ml (4 fl oz / ^{1}/$_2$ cup)
Salt a pinch

Preparation

1. Prepare batter. Combine all batter ingredients in a deep bowl and whisk into a smooth batter. Set aside.

2. Prepare marinade. Heat oil in a heavy saucepan. Add all marinade ingredients and sauté over medium heat until spices have softened. Set aside for a few minutes.

3. When cool enough to handle, place sautéed spices in a stone mortar and grind into a fine paste.

4. Combine vegetables and marinade in a bowl and mix well. Pour the mixture into the bowl of batter.

5. Heat oil for deep-frying in a pan over medium heat. Place 1 heaped Tbsp battered vegetable mixture into oil and fry very slowly until golden. Drain on paper towels.

6. In Bali, fried vegetable patties are served with pickled vegetables and whole green bird's eye chillies.

Fried Vegetable Fritters
Goreng-Gorengan

Ingredients

Cassava (tapioca) or sweet potatoes 400 g
    (14$^1/_3$ oz), peeled and sliced
Fermented soy bean cake (*tempe*) or firm tofu
    400 g (14$^1/_3$ oz)
Salt a pinch
Rice flour 50 g (1$^2/_3$ oz)
Vegetable oil for deep-frying

Batter

Cake flour 250 g (9 oz)
Rice flour 100 g (3$^1/_3$ oz)
Water 250 ml (8 fl oz / 1 cup)
Salt a pinch

Preparation

1. Prepare batter. Whisk batter ingredients together until smooth. Set aside.

2. Season cassava or sweet potatoes, fermented soy bean cake or tofu with salt and dust with rice flour.

3. Heat oil for deep-frying over medium heat.

4. Dip individual pieces of cassava or sweet potatoes, fermented soy bean cake or tofu into batter, then allow excess batter to drip off.

5. Deep-fry pieces in medium hot oil until golden. Cook in batches. Set aside to drain on paper towels.

6. In Bali, fried vegetable fritters are served with a dip made from sweet soy sauce and light soy sauce in the ration 2 : 3, laced with a generous amount of chopped bird's eye chillies.

Rujak

One of the most popular snacks in Bali, and indeed, in all of Indonesia, is *rujak*, sometimes also known as *petis*. It is a mixture of crisp unripe fruit, sliced and served with a sweet and sour sauce. With such a dish, unripe fruit and fruit with an inferior taste can be rendered surprisingly delectable. Although *rujak* is almost always available from push-cart vendors in the village, many also enjoy making them using fruit from their own fruit trees.

When making *rujak*, it is best to use crisp fruit to give the dish its proper texture. Unripe mangoes are a favourite. While wild mangoes tend to be stringy and have an unpleasant taste when ripe, using them in *rujak* turns the fruit into a piquant snack, with its less-than-ideal taste masked by the spicy sauce. Two relatives of mango, the *pakel* horse mango and *wani binjai,* also have inferior tastes, but are cheap and taste good when used in *rujak*.

Fruit like water apple (*nyamby biji*) and guava are naturally crisp when ripe, and are often tossed into this dish. Other popular fruit include the tuber, *bangkuan*—which is similar to jicama or yam bean— cucumbers and unripe papaya.

Vegetable & Fruit Salad in Sweet Tamarind Sauce
Rujak

Ingredients

Pineapple 75 g (2²/₃ oz), peeled and sliced

Green mango 75 g (2²/₃ oz), peeled and sliced

Green papaya 75 g (2²/₃ oz), peeled, seeded and sliced

Cucumber 75 g (2²/₃ oz), peeled, halved, seeded and sliced

Water apple or starfruit 75 g (2²/₃ oz), cut in quarters

Hikkoman, jicama or yam bean 75 g (2²/₃ oz), peeled and sliced

Sauce

Palm sugar 125 g (4¹/₂ oz)

Dried prawn (shrimp) paste (*terasi*) 1 tsp, roasted and crumbled

Bird's eye chillies 4–6, according to taste, finely sliced

Tamarind pulp 100 g (3¹/₃ oz), soaked in 125 ml (4 fl oz / ¹/₂ cup) warm water for 15 minutes, then strained; reserve tamarind liquid

Salt to taste

Preparation

1. Prepare sauce. Place palm sugar, prawn paste and chillies in a stone mortar or food processor and grind to a fine paste. Slowly blend in tamarind liquid into a smooth sauce. Season to taste with salt.

2. Place fruit and vegetables in a deep bowl. Drizzle over sauce and toss. Serve.

The Jaja Warung

There is rarely a neighbourhood that does not have a coffee and *jaja warung* where men gather in the morning to have a snack and discuss the latest gossip. The proprietors of these little stalls make two or three kinds of cakes (*jaja*) before sunrise and these are normally sold out before midday.

In many ways, all *jaja* taste similar as they all contain the same three basic ingredients. There is rice which holds the *jaja* together, coconut for flavouring and palm sugar for sweetening. A snack, a sweet, a bite for any time of the day, *jaja* are cakes which feature greatly in every part of Balinese life—from important ceremonies to a snatched moment of leisure. Practically all social functions require the presence of *jaja* as a snack. When you arrive at a Balinese wedding or a tooth filling ceremony for instance, you will always be handed a cardboard box containing an assortment of *jaja* and a bottle of soda or sweet tea. You find itinerant *jaja* vendors hawking their ware in front of every school and government office, at every sporting event, movie or political rally, and you'll meet them again at the most remote cock or cricket fight (necessarily out of the way because they are illegal!) to provide refreshment. When you are at the Barong show in Batubulan, your driver and guide would be eating *jaja* and drinking coffee in the *warung* out in front. During religious ceremonies, the street in front of every temple would be full of *jaja* sellers. After the offerings have been dedicated to the gods and carried home on the heads of the village ladies, the first thing the children will do is to eat whichever type of *jaja* is available. The chickens get the rest.

Coffee Culture

Coffee goes hand in hand with *jaja* as the drink of choice when snacking. It is by far the most popular beverage in Bali and it is not unusual to see even little children having coffee right alongside their parents. So widespread is coffee drinking that the colloquial word for 'drink' in Balinese is *ngwedang*, which is universally understood to mean "drink coffee".

Coffee here is usually purchased at the local market by weight and packed neatly in plastic bags. Balinese coffee consists mainly of Robusta beans which contain up to three times the amount of caffeine than Arabica beans. The flavour is often rather smoky, with a unique and rough coffee flavour. (Arabica is grown in Bali, but most of it is exported.) The beans are normally processed near the centres of production and shipped to Denpasar or other cities in large sacks. Small factories then roast the beans and grind them into a fine powder, to which is often added ground and roasted corn or rice. The result is a very fine powder that looks almost like the instant coffee we find in supermarkets around the world. However, much of it does not dissolve. As such, Balinese coffee is usually served with a spoon, so that the sediment can be stirred up periodically to flavour the coffee before drinking.

Coffee is always served in a simple glass without a handle. A spoonful of coffee powder and two spoonfuls of granulated white sugar are added to the glass, followed by hot water poured from a thermos flask. The Balinese like their coffee very sweet, and often without milk. If you do not want sugar in your coffee, say, "*Singmisi gula*", which means "without sugar". Otherwise lots of sugar will be added as it is the norm. When you have finished your coffee, expect to see a considerable amount of sediment at the bottom of the glass. While most Balinese do not add milk to their coffee, most *warungs* will have it in the form of sweetened condensed milk. Coffee with this milk added is called "*kopi susu*". Interestingly, when you see a local drinking his coffee with milk, you can be certain that the person is not originally from Bali but from another part of Indonesia, most likely Java.

While we're on the topic of snacking, here is a note on local etiquette: If you encounter a friend having a snack in a *warung*, he will almost invariably ask, "*Sampun ngewedang*?" ("Have you already had coffee?") In asking this question, he is merely being polite. He may not necessarily mean to ask you to join him to drink or snack, for such activities, you should remember, are marked by great formality in Bali. In asking the question, he is more likely just excusing himself for eating and drinking before you do, which would be considered rude. What the friend really means is: "Pardon me for eating and drinking while you are not doing so. I hope you already have had your food and drink." In answer to this polite greeting, one should simply reply, "*Sampun*", meaning in effect, "I have already eaten" (even if you may not have done so). This then puts the friend at ease for possibly having inadvertently broken a rule of etiquette.

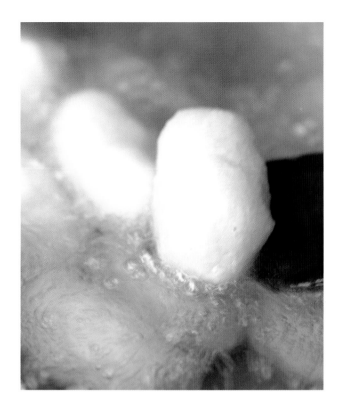

Street Snacks

Jimbaran Seafood Safes 13

Spiced Layer Cake
Kueh Lapis

Ingredients

Butter 300 g (10 oz)

Icing (confectioner's) sugar 250 g (9 oz)

Plain (all-purpose) flour 180 g (6½ oz)

Egg yolks 20

Sweetened condensed milk 100 ml (3½ fl oz / 6 Tbsp)

Egg whites 10

Spice Mix

Ground cinnamon 3 Tbsp

Ground cloves 2 Tbsp

Ground nutmeg 1 Tbsp

Ground cardamom 1 Tbsp

Ground fennel 2 tsp

Preparation

1. Preheat oven to 180°C (350°F). Line a 20-cm (8-in) square baking tin with greaseproof paper. Brush paper lightly with melted butter, then dust lightly with flour.

2. Combine butter and 150 g (5⅓ oz) icing sugar in a mixing bowl and beat until creamy and fluffy.

3. Gradually add egg yolks and condensed milk and continue to beat until batter is smooth.

4. In a separate bowl, combine egg whites and remaining icing sugar and whisk until egg whites are firm and stiff.

5. In a separate bowl, combine spices for spice mix and set aside.

6. Using a rubber spatula, lightly fold egg white mixture into egg yolk mixture.

7. Add 2 Tbsp spice mix and mix well.

8. Spread 100 ml (3½ fl oz / 6 Tbsp) cake mix evenly onto baking tin. Bake for 3–4 minutes until surface of batter is golden brown.

9. Spread another 100 ml (3½ fl oz / 6 Tbsp) batter evenly over cooked cake layer and bake for another 3–4 minutes until surface is golden brown.

10. Repeat steps 8 and 9 until batter is used up and cake is well baked.

11. Set aside to cool, then cut into even slices to serve.

Steamed Cassava Cakes
Getuk

Ingredients

Cassava (tapioca) 1 kg (2 lb 3 oz), peeled and cut
   into 3-cm (1½-in) cubes

Sugar 250 g (9 oz)

Butter 60 g (2 oz)

Vanilla essence ¼ tsp

Salt a pinch

Grated coconut 1 cup

Preparation

1. Steam cassava cubes until soft. Cool to room temperature.

2. Mash with sugar, butter, vanilla essence and salt. Mix well.

3. Push this mixture through a meat grinder fitted with a medium blade (same used for hamburgers) 3 times.

4. When pushing mixture out of grinder the third time, gently pull strands out, being careful not to break them. Place on a clean cutting board.

5. With a plastic knife, divide strands into even, pieces about 8-cm (3-in) long.

6. Top each piece with 1 tsp freshly grated coconut and serve.

Baked Rice Flour Cakes
Carabikang

Ingredients

Cake flour 250 g (9 oz)

Rice flour 500 g (1 lb 1½ oz)

Tapioca flour 200 g (7 oz)

Sugar 300 g (10 oz)

Eggs 2

Salt a pinch

Vanilla essence ¼ tsp

Coconut milk 1 litre (32 fl oz / 4 cups) + 250 ml
(8 fl oz / 1 cup)

Green food colouring 5 drops

Red food colouring 5 drops

Preparation

1. Combine cake, rice and tapioca flours in a bowl.
2. Mix sugar, eggs, vanilla essence and salt together in another bowl.
3. Combine flour and egg mixtures and blend well.
4. Gradually whisk in 1 litre (32 fl oz / 4 cups) coconut milk to get a smooth batter with a consistency that resembles a thick pancake mix.
5. Divide remaining 250 ml (8 fl oz / 1 cup) coconut milk into 2 bowls. Mix green food colouring into one bowl and red colouring into the other.
6. Heat a special rice flour cake brass mould over an open gas flame until very hot. Pour batter into the mould until three-quarters full.
7. Cook over medium heat until cakes start to dry up. Drop 1 tsp green and 1 tsp red coconut milk into the centre of cake and continue to cook until done.
8. Remove cakes from mould and press them from the bottom so they 'open up' like a flower.
9. If you don't have the brass mould, use a muffin mould. Bake in a preheated oven at 180°C (350°F) for 15 minutes or until the cakes are light and fluffy, dropping in the colouring 2–3 minutes before the cakes are done.
10. Serve at room temperature.

Jaja

Every market in Bali has several stalls filled with a large selection of colourful and unique-looking cakes. Ranging from bright green to pink and chocolate brown, they are packaged in all sorts of stunning wrappings in which the cakes are steamed. These stalls are manned by ladies who each would sell only a small selection of *jaja* which they prepare at home the night before.

While many of us would associate cakes to confections like chocolate cakes, Black Forest and Linzer torte, Balinese *jaja* are different—they are never baked, seldom prepared with milk and butter, and are mostly rice-based. Like most Asian sweets, they are fried, steamed or boiled.

Indeed, most *jaja* are made from rice. This should come as no surprise in a country where rice is abundant and is, after all, overwhelmingly the staple food. There are two important varieties of rice that are used in *jaja*— ordinary rice such as that used for everyday meals, and sticky or glutinous rice which is almost exclusively used for making *jaja*. Black rice is also widely used in *jaja*-making.

Black rice is never cooked on its own but mixed with a portion of glutinous white rice. It is usually either steamed or boiled and takes a longer time to cook compared to white rice, and must therefore be soaked overnight in cold water before cooking. Sometimes a knob of bruised ginger or a stalk of pandan leaf is added, and removed when the cooking is complete.

Bubuh

Besides rice and rice flour, pulses such as mung beans (*kacang ijo*) also feature prominently in *jaja*, in the form of porridges known as *bubuh*. When the starchy grain has been boiled in water to reach the desired consistency, various flavourings and even colouring is added. Among these are palm sugar (*gula barak*), grated coconut (*nyuh makikih*) and sometimes a colouring agent that also adds flavour. The favourite colouring additive is the leaf of the *kayu sugih* plant. The leaves are kneaded in a little water and a squeeze of lime is added to take away the 'green leafy' taste. Added to *bubuh*, or other foods, this produces a pleasant green colour and a light floral fragrance.

Mung bean soup (*bubuh kacang ijo*) may be served with black rice porridge (*bubuh injin*), which some push-cart vendors offer as a side dish.

Coconut Cakes
Kueh Batu Durian

Ingredients

Glutinous rice flour 500 g (1 lb 1$^{1}/_{2}$ oz) + more for dusting

Grated coconut 400 g (14$^{1}/_{3}$ oz)

Vanilla essence $^{1}/_{2}$ tsp

Salt a pinch

Vegetable oil for deep-frying

Sugar 200 g (7 oz)

Water 100 ml (3$^{1}/_{2}$ fl oz / 6 Tbsp)

Vinegar 1 tsp

Preparation

1. Combine glutinous rice flour, grated coconut, vanilla essence and salt and mix into a dough. Dough should be elastic and rather hard in consistency.

2. Shape dough into individual dumplings about 30 g (1 oz) each using your hands.

3. Heat oil for deep-frying over medium heat. Deep-fry dumplings over medium heat until golden. Do this in batches. Drain on paper towels.

4. In a heavy saucepan, combine sugar, water and vinegar and cook slowly over medium heat into a golden caramel.

5. Toss dumplings one at a time into caramel. Coat well.

6. Dust dumplings lightly with rice flour and serve.

Potato Cakes
Kueh Lumpur

Ingredients

Potatoes 500 g (1 lb 1$^{1}/_{2}$ oz), peeled and cut into 3-cm (1$^{1}/_{4}$-in) cubes

Margarine or butter 200 g (7 oz), melted

Eggs 3

Sugar 300 g (10 oz)

Vanilla essence 1 tsp

Rum essence 1 tsp

Coconut milk 1 litre (32 fl oz / 4 cups)

Cake flour 500 g (1 lb 1$^{1}/_{2}$ oz)

Raisins 100 g (3$^{1}/_{3}$ oz)

Young coconut flesh 250 g (9 oz), sliced, optional

Preparation

1. Steam potatoes until soft. Set aside to cool to room temperature.

2. Combine all ingredients except flour, raisins and coconut in a food processor and blend into a smooth, runny batter.

3. Pour batter into a mixing bowl and gradually whisk in flour, making sure batter is smooth and free of lumps. Strain through a sieve.

4. Preheat a special brass potato cake mould over an open flame. Fill the heated moulds three-quarters full with batter and allow to cook.

5. When cooked, turn cakes out of mould and set aside to cool.

6. If you don't have the brass mould, use a muffin mould. Bake in a preheated oven at 180°C (350°F) for 15 minutes or until cakes are done.

7. Garnish with raisins and coconut meat, if desired.

From top: Coconut Cakes, Potato Cakes

Fried Bananas

Fried bananas are enjoyed all over Asia. In Bali, fried bananas are called *gegodoh biu*. *Biu dangsaba* is the preferred variety of banana for this purpose.

Slices of peeled banana are dipped into a batter made of rice flour, to which water containing a little lime is added. They are then fried in coconut oil until golden brown. These snacks are sold in every market, *warung*, and always at the little itinerant stalls that are set up around some public attraction, like a cock fight, dance, *wayang*, or temple ceremony. The larger markets have stalls that specialise solely in fried bananas.

The word *gegodoh* is a general one and refers to all manner of fruit or starchy vegetables which have been first dipped in batter, then fried into a delectable snack. Sweet potatoes, breadfruit, jackfruit and bananas are commonly prepared this way, and go by the names *godoh kesela, godoh sukun, godoh nangka* and *godoh biu* respectively. They are delicious when freshly made and warm, but they can keep relatively well and are often simply stacked on a plate in *warungs* for customers who will come throughout the day.

Fruit Fritters
Buah Buahan Goreng

Ingredients

Assorted fruit (banana, jackfruit, pineapple, mango) 400 g (14^1/$_3$ oz), peeled and sliced

Rice flour for dusting 50 g (1^2/$_3$ oz)

Vegetable oil for deep-frying

Batter

Cake flour 125 g (4^1/$_2$ oz)

Rice flour 50 g (1^2/$_3$ oz)

Water 125 ml (4 fl oz / ^{1}/$_2$ cup)

Sugar 1 Tbsp

Salt a pinch

Dipping Sauce

Palm sugar 200 g (6^1/$_2$ oz), chopped

Water 75 ml (2 fl oz / ^{1}/$_4$ cup and 1 Tbsp)

Pandan leaf 1, bruised

Preparation

1. Combine all the batter ingredients in a deep bowl and whisk into a smooth batter, slightly runny batter.

2. Dust fruit with rice flour, then dip them into the batter, one at a time.

3. Fry fruit in medium hot oil (160°C / 325°F) until golden and crisp. (Be sure to fry only a few slices at a time to prevent the oil from cooling. When heating the oil, make sure the temperature of the oil rises gradually.) Drain fruit on paper towels to soak up the excess oil.

4. To make the dipping sauce, place palm sugar, water and pandan leaves in a saucepan, and bring the mixture to a boil. Let it simmer until sauce is lightly thickened. Set aside to cool.

5. Serve palm sugar sauce in a separate bowl as a dip for the fried fruit.

Black Rice Pudding
Bubuh Injin

Ingredients

Black glutinous rice 250 g (9 oz)
White glutinous rice 75 g (2²/₃ oz)
Water 1.5 litres (48 fl oz / 6 cups)
Pandan leaf 1
Palm sugar 125 g (4¹/₂ oz)
Salt a pinch
Coconut milk 375 ml (12 fl oz / 1¹/₂ cups)

Preparation

1. Rinse black and white glutinous rice under running water, then soak in plenty of tepid water overnight. Drain before using.

2. Place 750 ml (24 fl oz / 3 cups) water, black and white glutinous rice and pandan leaf into a heavy pan and simmer over medium heat for 45 minutes. Top up with water as necessary.

3. Add palm sugar and continue to cook until most of the liquid has evaporated.

4. Season with a pinch of salt. Remove from heat, and let cool.

5. Serve at room temperature, topped with coconut milk.

Mung Bean Soup
Bubuh Kacang Ijo

This delicious breakfast dish is similar to an Italian risotto, lightly runny, with the beans just done. It is very popular during the hot afternoon hours served with a generous amount of shaved ice and sweetened condensed milk.

Ingredients

Mung beans 350 g (12 oz)

Water 1.5 litres (48 fl oz / 6 cups)

Ginger 50 g (1$^2/_3$ oz), peeled, sliced and crushed

Coconut milk 500 ml (16 fl oz / 2 cups)

Palm sugar 125 g (4$^1/_2$ oz)

Salt a pinch

Preparation

1. Rinse mung beans thoroughly under running water to remove husks and impurities.

2. If you like, heighten the flavour of the beans by heating them briefly in a heavy pan without oil over medium heat. This will add a slightly roasted flavour to the beans, but be careful not to burn them.

3. Place beans in a heavy saucepan and add water and ginger. Bring to a boil, then lower heat and simmer for about 30 minutes or until beans are almost done. Add more water as required.

4. Stir in coconut milk, palm sugar and salt and simmer for another 10 minutes until beans are soft but not overcooked. Remove from heat.

5. In Bali, this mung bean soup is either served at room temperature topped with grated coconut and coconut milk, or chilled and served with ice cubes or shaved ice.

Sticky Rice Dumplings with Palm Sugar
Klepon

Ingredients

Glutinous rice flour 300 g (10 oz)

Salt a pinch

Warm water 125 ml (4 fl oz / $^1/_2$ cup)

Suji **leaves** 50 g (1$^2/_3$ oz), sliced

Pandan leaves 3, sliced

Palm sugar 150 g (5$^1/_3$ oz), finely grated

Grated coconut 150 g (5 oz), steamed

Preparation

1. Place glutinous rice flour and salt in a bowl and mix well.

2. Combine water, suji and pandan leaves in another bowl and knead well to extract as much flavour and colour as possible from the leaves. If suji leaves are not available, substitute with more pandan leaves.

3. Gradually add this liquid to rice flour mixture while kneading the dough, until dough can be shaped.

4. Pull out small portions of dough and shape into little balls. Flatten them with a teaspoon.

5. Place $^1/_2$ tsp palm sugar into the centre of the flattened dough, then fold the sides of the dough over to encase sugar. Reshape into balls.

6. Bring a large pot of water to the boil. Lower heat to simmer, then place dumplings in and cook until dumplings float. Remove dumplings with a slotted spoon. Set aside to drain.

7. Roll dumplings in grated coconut and serve.

Rice Flour Dumplings in Palm Sugar Coconut Sauce
Jaja Batun Bedil

Ingredients

Grated coconut 150 g (5⅓ oz), steamed

Rice Flour Dumplings

Glutinous rice flour 150 g (5⅓ oz / 1 cup)
Tapioca flour 75 g (2⅔ oz / ½ cup)
Water 180 ml (6 fl oz / ¾ cup)
Salt a pinch

Sauce

Water 125 ml (4 fl oz / ½ cup)
Palm sugar 125 g (4½ oz), chopped
Pandan leaf 1, bruised
Salt a pinch

Preparation

1. Make rice flour dumplings. Place both flours and salt into a deep mixing bowl. Gradually add water and knead into a smooth dough. Dough should be soft and elastic.

2. Pinch out small portions of dough and roll into small balls about 1-cm (½-in) in diameter.

3. Bring 4 litres (128 fl oz / 16 cups) of lightly salted water to the boil. Add dumplings and return to the boil for 5 minutes. Drain dumplings and lower into iced water to cool.

4. Make sauce. Combine all sauce ingredients in a heavy saucepan and bring to a boil. Lower heat and simmer for 10 minutes.

5. Drop dumplings into simmering sauce and cook gently for 20 minutes.

6. Leave to cool in sauce before serving topped with grated coconut.

Rice Flour Pancakes with Palm Sugar & Coconut
Laklak

Ingredients

Rice flour 300 g (10 oz)
Water 100 ml (3¹/₂ fl oz / 6 Tbsp)
Salt a pinch
Grated coconut 100 g (3¹/₃ oz)

Palm Sugar Syrup

Palm sugar 150 g (5¹/₃ oz), chopped
Water 100 ml (3¹/₂ fl oz / 6 Tbsp)
Pandan leaf 1, tied into a knot

Preparation

1. Prepare pancakes. Place rice flour and salt into a mixing bowl. Add water gradually and work with a wooden spoon into a smooth batter.

2. Heat a little oil in a non-stick pan. Spoon in 1 Tbsp batter, tilting pan to spread batter.

3. Cook pancake until is golden on one side and very lightly brown on the other. Lift it carefully off pan and set aside.

4. Repeat until batter is used up.

5. Prepare sauce. Combine sauce ingredients in a heavy saucepan and simmer until it thickens lightly. Set aside to cool to room temperature. Discard pandan leaf.

6. To serve, sprinkle pancakes with grated coconut and drizzle over with palm sugar syrup.

Fruit Cocktail
Es Campur

Ingredients

Palm sugar 375 g (13 oz), chopped

Water 250 ml (8 fl oz / 1 cup)

Pandan leaf 1, bruised and knotted

Sweet potato 50 g ($1^2/_3$ oz), peeled and cut into small cubes

Palm fruit 200 g (7 oz)

Fruit (pineapple, mango, jackfruit, banana) 200 g (7 oz), peeled and diced

Rice flour dumplings (page 152) 1 quantity, coloured with food colouring, if desired (see Note)

Coconut milk 4 Tbsp

Lime juice 2 Tbsp

Preparation

1. Place palm sugar, water and pandan leaf in a pan. Bring to a boil, then lower heat and simmer for 5 minutes.

2. Add sweet potato and palm fruit and simmer until sweet potato is almost soft.

3. Add diced fruit and dumplings and return to a boil. Simmer for another 2 minutes.

4. Stir in coconut milk and let it and simmer for another minute. Drizzle over with lime juice. Set aside to cool.

5. Serve fruit cocktail at room temperature or chilled with ice.

NOTE

To colour the dumplings, add a few drops of food colouring of choice to the dough and knead until the dough is evenly coloured.

Banana or Avocado Juice
Es Pisang dan Es Apokat

Ingredients

Bananas or avocados 400 g (14$^1/_3$ oz), peeled and diced

Milk 400 ml (13 fl oz / 1$^3/_4$ cups)

Natural yoghurt 200 ml (6$^1/_2$ fl oz / $^4/_5$ cup)

Lime juice 2 Tbsp

Preparation

1. Place all ingredients, except lime juice, in a food processor. If you like, add some ice as well, and blend until creamy and smooth.

2. Add lime juice and serve cold.

Glossary of
Ingredients

Candlenuts
This is a brittle, waxy yellowish nut that is similar in appearance to the macadamia nut. It is used as a binding agent and adds a faint flavour to dishes. If not available, use shelled and skinned raw peanuts.

Chillies
The Balinese love using chilli in their food and often use an excessive amount. Three types of chillies are used and the level of heat increases as the size decreases. Always wear gloves when handling chillies and wash hands and all surfaces in contact with the chillies thoroughly thereafter.

Chillies, large, red
These finger-size chillies are by far the mildest chillies found in Bali. They are mainly used for flavouring and are always seeded before use. Most recipes in this book make use of these chillies. If the chillies you use are hot, reduce the quantity by one-third.

Chillies, small
This short, fat chilli is only about 2.5-cm (1-in) long and it is the most favoured and commonly used chilli. They are normally chopped or bruised before use, adding a good spicy kick to the dishes prepared.

Clove
The clove tree is a member of the myrtle family and is native to Southeast Asia. The central mountain ranges of Bali are full of this very pretty reddish coloured tree. The spice is the unopened flower bud. When dried, it turns a reddish-brown colour and becomes one of the strongest smelling spices.

Coriander seeds
This dried spice is commonly used in Balinese cooking. They are crushed before use which imparts a much stronger flavour.

Galangal
This large rhizome is a standard ingredient in Balinese cooking. It is known as *laos* in Indonesia and greater galangal in English.
It is available fresh or in powder form in many Asian shops and supermarkets.

Ginger
The rhizome of an attractive flowering plant, ginger is widely used in Balinese cooking. Ginger should be plump and firm. Peel then either slice or pound before using. It is easily available in Asian stores and should never be substituted with ground ginger.

Kaffir limes
This small green citrus fruit is often used in small quantities in Balinese cooking. The fruit has a marked protrusion on one end and its skin is knobbly and wrinkled. Its taste ranges from sour to bitter and the Balinese prefer it to any other type of lime. The common lime found in most Asian shops makes an acceptable substitute.

Kaffir lime leaf
The kaffir lime leaf looks like two leaves joined end to end and it is used whole in soups and sauces or finely chopped for fish, duck and chicken dishes.

Lemon basil
This delicate herb has a very pleasant citrus flavour and is mostly used with fish dishes cooked in banana leaves. Regular basil can be used as a substitute.

Lemon grass
A common ingredient in Balinese cooking, lemon grass must be peeled and lightly bruised before use, or bruised and very finely sliced. When used to flavour spice paste or sauce, bruise it along the whole length and tie into a knot. This will prevent the lemon grass fibres from falling apart. If lemon grass is unavailable, use lemon or lime zests.

Lesser galangal
This small rhizome is a standard ingredient in Balinese cooking. It is called *kencur* in Indonesia and is available in powder form. If unavailable, replace the amount required in a recipe with an equal amount of ginger and galangal.

Nutmeg
This aromatic sweet spice is mostly used with strong flavoured meats such as duck and lamb. Avoid using ready-ground nutmeg as it loses its flavour readily. Instead, grate whole nutmeg just before it is needed.

Palm sugar
Sold in cylindrical or round cakes, palm sugar is obtained by boiling the liquid extracted from the unopened flower bud of some palm trees, such as the sugar palm in Bali or the coconut tree in Java. In the northeastern part of Bali, palm sugar is made from the Lontar Palm.

Pandan leaf
The aromatic leaf of a type of almost thornless pandanus, the screwpine leaf is used for flavouring cakes and snacks. The shredded leaf is also a common topping on offering baskets in Bali.

Peanuts

When choosing raw peanuts, look for those with the skin still on. Peanuts are tastier and more flavoursome when they are deep-fried or roasted in their skins. The second best thing is peanuts which are roasted in the shell. These are available in most supermarkets.

Pepper

In Balinese cooking, black pepper is more popularly used than white pepper. Grind or crush fresh peppercorns for the best flavour, as ground pepper loses its aroma quickly.

Prawn (shrimp) paste, dried

Made by drying prawns under the sun and then pounding them into a pulp, this pungent paste is available in small packages from the market. Grill or roast without oil before using. Roasted prawn paste can be stored for several months in an airtight container. Although pungent, prawn paste adds a pleasant flavour when used in dishes.

Salam leaf

The *salam* leaf is used to flavour soups, stews, vegetable and meat dishes. Although similar to the bay leaf in use and appearance, they are completely different and should not be used as substitutes for each other.

Shallots

The common onion available in Bali is small and red, and just slightly different from shallots sold in other parts of the world. If this type of shallot is not available, replace with red Spanish onions.

Tamarind

The tamarind seed pod ripens on the tree. It contains a fleshy pulp, which has a very sour taste. The pulp needs to be soaked in warm water for 15 minutes, then strained through a fine sieve. The seed and fibres are then discarded. Only the juice is used. Tamarind is widely available in their pods or compressed, minus pods and seeds.

Turmeric

An attractive perennial with large lily-like leaves and yellow flowers, turmeric is a member of the ginger family and, like ginger, it is an underground rhizome of the plant. The brownish skin must be scraped or peeled to expose the bright yellow flesh. If fresh turmeric is not available, substitute 1 Tbsp ground turmeric for 100 g (3$^1/_3$ oz) fresh roots.

Weights & Measures

Quantities for this book are given in Metric and American (spoon) measures. Standard spoon measurements used are: 1 tsp = 5 ml and 1 Tbsp = 15 ml. All measures are level unless otherwise stated.

LIQUID AND VOLUME MEASURES

Metric	Imperial	American
5 ml	1/6 fl oz	1 teaspoon
10 ml	1/3 fl oz	1 dessertspoon
15 ml	1/2 fl oz	1 tablespoon
60 ml	2 fl oz	1/4 cup (4 tablespoons)
85 ml	2 1/2 fl oz	1/3 cup
90 ml	3 fl oz	3/8 cup (6 tablespoons)
125 ml	4 fl oz	1/2 cup
180 ml	6 fl oz	3/4 cup
250 ml	8 fl oz	1 cup
300 ml	10 fl oz (1/2 pint)	1 1/4 cups
375 ml	12 fl oz	1 1/2 cups
435 ml	14 fl oz	1 3/4 cups
500 ml	16 fl oz	2 cups
625 ml	20 fl oz (1 pint)	2 1/2 cups
750 ml	24 fl oz (1 1/5 pints)	3 cups
1 litre	32 fl oz (1 3/5 pints)	4 cups
1.25 litres	40 fl oz (2 pints)	5 cups
1.5 litres	48 fl oz (2 2/5 pints)	6 cups
2.5 litres	80 fl oz (4 pints)	10 cups

OVEN TEMPERATURE

	°C	°F	Gas Regulo
Very slow	120	250	1
Slow	150	300	2
Moderately slow	160	325	3
Moderate	180	350	4
Moderately hot	190/200	370/400	5/6
Hot	210/220	410/440	6/7
Very hot	230	450	8
Super hot	250/290	475/550	9/10

LENGTH

Metric	Imperial
0.5 cm	1/4 inch
1 cm	1/2 inch
1.5 cm	3/4 inch
2.5 cm	1 inch

DRY MEASURES

Metric	Imperial
30 grams	1 ounce
45 grams	1 1/2 ounces
55 grams	2 ounces
70 grams	2 1/2 ounces
85 grams	3 ounces
100 grams	3 1/2 ounces
110 grams	4 ounces
125 grams	4 1/2 ounces
140 grams	5 ounces
280 grams	10 ounces
450 grams	16 ounces (1 pound)
500 grams	1 pound, 1 1/2 ounces
700 grams	1 1/2 pounds
800 grams	1 3/4 pounds
1 kilogram	2 pounds, 3 ounces
1.5 kilograms	3 pounds, 4 1/2 ounces
2 kilograms	4 pounds, 6 ounces

ABBREVIATION

tsp	teaspoon
Tbsp	tablespoon
g	gramme
kg	kilogramme
ml	millilitre